Whatever Happened to Pudding Pops?

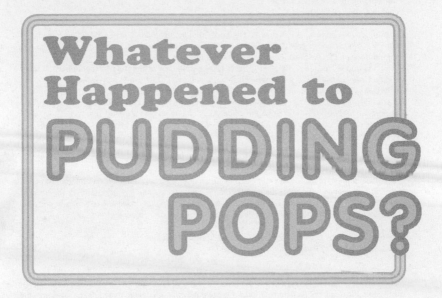

Whatever Happened to PUDDING POPS?

The Lost Toys, Tastes & Trends of the '70s & '80s

GAEL FASHINGBAUER COOPER
and BRIAN BELLMONT

A Perigee Book

A PERIGEE BOOK
Published by the Penguin Group
Penguin Group (USA) Inc.
375 Hudson Street, New York, New York 10014, USA
Penguin Group (Canada), 90 Eglinton Avenue East, Suite 700, Toronto, Ontario M4P 2Y3, Canada
(a division of Pearson Penguin Canada Inc.)
Penguin Books Ltd., 80 Strand, London WC2R 0RL, England
Penguin Group Ireland, 25 St. Stephen's Green, Dublin 2, Ireland (a division of Penguin Books Ltd.)
Penguin Group (Australia), 250 Camberwell Road, Camberwell, Victoria 3124, Australia
(a division of Pearson Australia Group Pty. Ltd.)
Penguin Books India Pvt. Ltd., 11 Community Centre, Panchsheel Park, New Delhi—110 017, India
Penguin Group (NZ), 67 Apollo Drive, Rosedale, Auckland 0632, New Zealand
(a division of Pearson New Zealand Ltd.)
Penguin Books (South Africa) (Pty.) Ltd., 24 Sturdee Avenue, Rosebank, Johannesburg 2196, South Africa
Penguin Books Ltd., Registered Offices: 80 Strand, London WC2R 0RL, England

While the authors have made every effort to provide accurate telephone numbers and Internet addresses at the time of publication, neither the publisher nor the authors assume any responsibility for errors or for changes that occur after publication. Further, the publisher does not have any control over and does not assume any responsibility for author or third-party websites or their content.

Copyright © 2011 by Gael Fashingbauer Cooper and Brian Bellmont
Text design by Tiffany Estreicher

First edition: June 2011

Library of Congress Cataloging-in-Publication Data

Cooper Gael Fashingbauer.
    Whatever happened to pudding pops? : the lost toys, tastes & trends of the '70s & '80s / Gael Fashingbauer Cooper and Brian Bellmont.—1st ed.
      p.   cm.
      Includes index.
      "A Perigee Book."
      ISBN 978-0-399-53671-7
      I. Popular culture—United States—History—20th century.   2. United States—Social life and customs—1971–   3. United States—Civilization—1970–   I. Bellmont, Brian.   II. Title.
E169.Z8C6556   2011
306.0973'09047—dc22   2010050677

PRINTED IN THE UNITED STATES OF AMERICA

10   9   8   7   6   5   4   3   2   1

To our parents,
Ann and Ed Fashingbauer and Bob and Karen Bellmont,
who let us watch the TV shows, eat the junk food, and play
with the toys that inspired this book.

To Rob Cooper and Jen Bellmont, our adored spouses,
who put up with so much while we worked on this project.

To our beloved daughters,
Kelly Cooper and Rory and Maddy Bellmont.
We can't wait to see the pop culture of your future!

And in memory of Ann Biales and David Walden.
You are missed.

INTRODUCTION

I F you owe a couple cavities to Pudding Pops and Marathon candy bars, learned your adverbs from *Schoolhouse Rock!*, ever spent a few of your birthdays at Shakey's Pizza, and can still imitate the slo-mo bionic running sound of the Six Million Dollar Man, this book is for you.

For a supposedly fractured generation, we kids of the 1970s and 1980s share a far more universal past than kids today. We all watched the same five channels, shopped at the same few chain stores, hummed the same commercial jingles. We may not remember the moon landing, but we remember Moon Boots. The Mystery Date board game didn't seem sexist, and exploding Pop Rocks were the epitome of candy science.

At school, everyone who didn't smell of Giorgio or Aramis reeked of Sun-In or Gee, Your Hair Smells Terrific. Our slides and jungle gyms were made of shin-burning metal with sharp edges, kids regularly looked things up in card catalogs, and learning how to change a typewriter ribbon still seemed like a good idea. We would have laughed at the thought of purchasing bottled water, and even the youngest among us were trusted to play with javelin-sharp lawn darts.

Those things didn't just dramatically vanish one day in a flurry of farewells and confetti. Childhoods don't end that way. Sure, there are marking points, like graduations and moving days, but they don't tell the whole story. The little things slip away every day, and most of them go without warning.

Some vanished totally, like Freakies cereal. Some stayed around but faded from the spotlight, like Sea-Monkeys or Shrinky Dinks. Others were replaced by better technology, like school filmstrips giving way to DVD players, or piles of vinyl records changing to eight-tracks, then to cassettes, then to CDs, and now to MP3s. Still others stuck around and earned places in the hearts of the next generation—have you seen how many varieties of Lip Smackers kids today can buy?

A LOT of people our age hate the label "Generation X," preferring to call themselves children of the 1970s and 1980s. Those are goofy decades to embrace, with their avocado refrigerators and wood-paneled rec rooms, their leg warmers and shoulder pads. But if you loved your childhood home even though it wasn't the most glamorous place on the block, you likely have fond memories of the years in which you grew up—no matter how goofy, no matter how clumsy. In a way, these two are decades only a native could take to heart.

It's not really the things that we loved; it's our memories of those things and how they fit into our lives. The orange-and-red shag carpeting in your bedroom isn't as important as the hours you spent trying to make your Lincoln Logs stand up on it. Malibu Barbie isn't necessarily the world's best doll, but if when you think of her you picture your cousin and remember how hard you laughed when her baby brother bit Barbie in the boob, then to you she is the best doll, now and for eternity.

"Life moves pretty fast," said our fellow 1980s child Ferris Bueller. "If you don't stop and look around once in a while, you could miss it." That's what we're trying to do in this book—stop and look around, close our eyes, and redecorate the rooms of our childhood. We want to remember the sounds we heard, the foods we ate, the toys that passed into our hands for a day or for a decade. We couldn't possibly write about everything, and if one of your favorites isn't here, rest assured we probably loved it, too; we just ran out of room and time. Not everything here was invented in the 1970s or 1980s, but everything listed was important to us in that time period and, perhaps, to you.

In addition to sharing specific childhood memories, we've assigned each item an X-tinction rating. They're pretty self-explanatory, but we include them as a way to bring our reminiscences up-to-date. Many things live on, others are gone for good, and some have had a makeover and been reintroduced in some way. Where we can, we note if a certain item has been completely replaced by something else.

So flip up the collar of that polo shirt and dig in. We're off on a guided tour through a childhood of lost memories, back to the days when MTV played music videos and Quisp and Quake duked it out for cereal supremacy. Memories are made of this.

After School Specials

A S preachy as Sunday school and as subtle as Gallagher, *After School Specials* tackled the juicy social issues, from divorce to date rape, that public schools in the '70s and '80s couldn't talk about. Watching these shows was like peeking at those books the people you babysat for kept hidden high on a bedroom shelf. But because they were dubbed "educational," you could watch completely guilt-free.

A Martian could figure out the plots from the titles alone: "Schoolboy Father." "Andrea's Story: A Hitchhiking Tragedy." "Please Don't Hit Me, Mom." "The Boy Who Drank Too Much." Who wouldn't rush home after algebra to tune in to these tawdry tales?

Hilariously, the scripts could have been written by a nun who didn't get out much. Every social issue was treated with the same amount of gravitas, be it shoplifting or Satanism. But the casts were like an all-star team of teen favorites. Rob Lowe and Dana Plato made a baby! Kristy McNichol couldn't get along with her stepdad! *After School Specials* were like the mall for kid actors: Eventually, you saw everyone there.

X-TINCTION RATING: Gone for good.

REPLACED BY: Made-for-TV movies come close, with titles like *Death of a Cheerleader*, *Too Young to Be a Dad*, and *Mother, May I Sleep with Danger?* But you can relive the real thing by picking up the original *After School Specials* on DVD, complete with school bus– and Trapper Keeper–shaped boxes.

Air Hockey

EVERYBODY knew one lucky kid who had an air hockey table in his rec room. These were often the same spoiled Richie Riches whose parents also bought them a pinball machine and full-sized popcorn cart. But who cared? For a day, they were our best friends, as long as they let us join in the Jetson-like wonder of this truly space-age sport.

Introduced in 1972, the oxygen-powered game put lower-tech basement activities like pool and Ping-Pong to shame. With the flip of a switch, the compressor would noisily shudder into action, firing air through tiny holes in the table and giving kids the power to levitate a tiny puck.

And then, blower-fueled ecstasy. The action was fast paced and airplane-bathroom loud. The mallet, which looked like a little sombrero, let kids whack the plastic puck with the intensity of a pint-sized Wayne Gretzky. The puck would click and clack as it banked off the sides until one killing blow would send it flying into the air—and into our opponent's orthodontia.

Dangerous? Sure. But a lifetime of chipped teeth was worth it for the few minutes we were walking—and playing hockey—on air.

X-TINCTION RATING: Still going strong. Air hockey has even become a competitive sport, under the auspices of the U.S. Air Hockey Association.

FUN FACT: A similar game called hover hockey uses a puck with a fan inside that produces its own airstream to float on, like a little *Star Wars* landspeeder.

Ants in the Pants

THE whole concept of Schaper's Ants in the Pants game was baffling. Were the red, yellow, green, and blue plastic bugs really supposed to be ants? We're not entomologists, but they looked a lot more like grasshoppers. And why were we trying to flick the ants into a pair of pants in the first place? For that matter, why were the pants and suspenders standing by themselves? And perhaps most importantly, whatever happened to the owner of the pants?

Schaper, which also made Cootie and Don't Break the Ice, never really answered those pressing questions, and kids didn't really care. All we wanted to do was fling bugs. In 1997, new owner Hasbro added a cardboard Dalmatian to the plastic pants-and-suspenders combo, which acted as a backboard. His pose is mocking, as if he's daring kids to just try and infest his britches with insects. Game on, dog. Don't let the ants hit you in the junk.

As much fun as it was, Ants in the Pants was really just a glorified version of tiddlywinks. Or, as beer-loving college students like to call it, Quarters.

X-TINCTION RATING: Still going strong.
FUN FACT: In a 1998 episode of *South Park*, Cartman, who was expecting a red Mega Man action figure as a birthday gift, was less than pleased to receive Ants in the Pants instead.

Atari 2600

F you could go back to the 1980s and show an Atari 2600–addicted kid a modern screenshot of Grand Theft Auto, it'd be like escorting Amelia Earhart onto the space shuttle.

Today, it's easy to snort at Atari's pixilated Pitfall Harry, swinging from a mighty jagged line. Pac-Man appeared to have been hastily copied from the legendary arcade version by a kid with no depth perception. But remember, until the 2600 came out, the pinnacle of home gaming was Pong, a black-and-white game in which small vertical lines beat up on a tiny square. The 2600 felt like the future.

The great games have passed into legend: Space Invaders. Asteroids. Frogger. But it's the bizarre ones that are forever burned into our brainpans. In Chase the Chuckwagon, you guided a dog to his product-placed Purina kibble. In Plaque Attack, you protected teeth

by shooting toothpaste at invading food. In Journey Escape, you guided members of the band Journey past groupies and crooked promoters to get them to their . . . spaceship?

Atari didn't go down easy. The 2600 was fourteen when it was officially retired in 1992. Back in the 1980s, its TV jingle demanded to know: "Have you played Atari today?" No, not today, but sometimes we think we would give up our HDTVs, our iPhones, even our hybrid cars for just one more hour sprawled on the living-room floor, helping that damned frog cross the road.

X-TINCTION RATING: Gone for good.
REPLACED BY: Intellivision, Super Nintendo, Xbox, take your pick. But the 2600 was so beloved that consoles dubbed "Atari Flashback" have been released, with original games and the same cheesy fake-wood paneling of their grandfather.

Australia Mania

ONE day, Americans couldn't tell Australia from Austria, and the next, we were all wearing clip-on koalas.

Olivia Newton-John may have started the trend playing Aussie babe Sandy in *Grease*, but it was Men at Work's 1981 hit "Down Under" that sealed the deal, smashing into our brains like a boomerang. Many folks never gained any more knowledge of this vast continent than what's contained in its lyrics, which were as bewildering as "Waltzing Matilda." A fried-out combie? Head full of zombie? Where men chunder? A Vegemite sandwich sounded good—that is, until we got our hands on the nasty spread and realized that eating it was kind of like licking a bouillon cube.

But for a while, adding the words "Down Under" or an Australian accent to almost anything upped its cool quotient to near Fonzie level. Disney mice *The Rescuers* had a *Down Under* sequel and so, oddly enough, did the girls from *Facts of Life*. Man, where was Crocodile Dundee and his enormous knife when you needed him? Thankfully, a dingo ate this trend somewhere around 1992.

X-TINCTION RATING: Gone for good.

REPLACED BY: One of the few remaining traces of the trend: the proliferation of Outback Steakhouses.

FUN FACT: According to IMDb.com, there were worries that Americans would think *"Crocodile" Dundee* was an animal film, so quotes were added around the word *Crocodile* when the film was released in the United States. Crikey, mates, we're not all drongos.

The Bad News Bears

IN the movies, kids were often portrayed as insufferable saintly little twits. Not so in *The Bad News Bears*. These foulmouthed brats much more closely resembled your own playground foes. Mouthy Tanner called his own teammates every slur in the book. Engelberg chomped chocolate while he was playing catcher. Ogilvie was a benchwarming nerd and Timmy Lupus an unabashed "booger-eating spaz." Add in lone girl Amanda, rebellious jock Kelly Leak, and alcoholic pool-cleaning coach Buttermaker (Walter Matthau, in the role he was born to play), and you had yourself a team.

The swearing, the slurs, and, best of all, a drunk Buttermaker driving the kids around, seat belt–free, ensured that this 1976 movie would never fully meet with parents' approval, making kids love it all the more. Who wouldn't want to be cigarette-smokin', Harley-ridin' Kelly Leak?

And the fact that the Bears lose it all in the end struck a true chord with your average bench-riding viewer. When Tanner tells the victorious Yankees to take their apology and their trophy and shove it, he's speaking for every fat, mouthy, booger-eatin' spaz in the audience. Play ball!

X-TINCTION RATING: Revived and revised.

REPLACED BY: The film was remade as *Bad News Bears* (inexplicably dropping the *The*) in 2005, with Billy Bob Thornton in the Matthau role.

FUN FACT: Reportedly, Kristy McNichol, Jodie Foster, and Sarah Jessica Parker were all considered for the role of Amanda, the part that went to Tatum O'Neal.

The Banana Splits Adventure Hour

THE *Banana Splits Adventure Hour* deserves a spot in Gen X heaven just for giving puppetmaster brothers Sid and Marty Krofft their start. Cartoon kings Bill Hanna and Joe Barbera hired the brothers to create costumes and sets for their psychedelic freak-out of a show about a gorilla, a beagle, an elephant, and a lion who hung out in a *Laugh-In*-styled clubhouse and sang horrifyingly bad bubblegum pop.

When not riding around in the kid-coveted "banana buggies," the Splits introduced cartoons, including *The Arabian Knights* and *The Three Musketeers* (sadly, not about the candy bar). Live-action serial *Danger Island* may have been optimistically named—the villain wore a not-so-threatening pink-polka-dotted bandana, and the only "danger" involved a cream-pie fight.

Banana Splits was most remembered for its bizarre catchphrases ("Uh-oh, Chongo!") and a seriously kick-ass theme song that was later covered by Liz Phair with Material Issue.

X-TINCTION RATING: Gone for good.

REPLACED BY: The original *Banana Splits* aired only from 1968 to 1970, but they keep showing up on TV. Cartoon Network revived it briefly in the 2000s with an even creepier costume for Snorky the elephant, and reruns pop up on Boomerang.

Bar None Candy Bar

BETAMAX was better than VHS, but we all know who won the VCR war. In the battle of cookie wafer–based candy bars, a similar upset occurred. The deliciously chocolatey, crunchy Bar None was taken down by an inferior bar, boring old Twix.

If Augustus Gloop had been holding a box of cookies when he fell into Willy Wonka's chocolate river, he might have invented Bar None. Introduced by Hershey in 1987, this candy had it all—a double-decker bunk bed of chocolate wafers lavishly spread with chocolate cream and peanuts and then doused in more chocolate.

The commercials went down a decidedly creepy road, showing Bar None as the only treat that could "tame the chocolate beasty." In one, a zookeeper-like guy throws Bar None to a growling unseen monster; in another, an ordinary woman grows super-disturbing, lumpy hands and feet until Bar None's chocolate soothes her.

But whether or not it cured monster feet, Bar None just didn't catch on with humans. Late in its life, Hershey even tried injecting it with caramel, in a sure act of Twix envy, but to no avail. It's as extinct as the chocolate beasty.

X-TINCTION RATING: Gone for good.
REPLACED BY: For a while, a retooled bar was available in Mexico, but that, too, appears to have said "adios."

Barrel of Monkeys

NO one ever said the tub of interconnecting chimps known as Barrel of Monkeys didn't live up to its blandly descriptive name. No fancy gimmicks, sounds, or complex rules. Do they dance? Do they chitter? Do they swing from trees? Nope. They hook arms, and that's it.

The little synthetic simians in Barrel of Monkeys are decidedly low-tech toys—and they live in a barrel, which probably smells. Their simplistic lifestyle is a little less exciting than that of real monkeys, who leap from tree branches, fling poo, and, at least on *B.J. and the Bear*, solve crimes.

The plastic primates' raison d'être is simple: to get you to try

to hook together a chain of the little guys. (Instruction #1: "Dump monkeys on table.") At least one researcher found a more advanced use: The National Institute for Medical Research in London used the monkeys to model "the geometry of multi–subunit protein structures." Apparently, the toy monkeys mimic molecules. Uh, sure. And they're also fun to play with. Well, not really. But anyone who's given it a try knows there's something primal and strangely compelling about making a chain of monkeys. It's more fun than—oh, you know.

X-TINCTION RATING: Still going strong.

FUN FACT: In a scene from 1995's *Toy Story*, the toys desperately try to rescue Buzz Lightyear by dangling a chain of monkeys out the window.

Battle of the Network Stars

IN the '70s, we didn't have TMZ.com, *US Weekly*, or *Extra*. Thank God for *Battle of the Network Stars*, which gave us a rare behind-the-scenes look at celebrities in their unguarded, natural setting. OK, not natural, exactly, unless kayak races are somehow part of Joan Van Ark's daily routine.

The two-hour specials pitted ABC vs. CBS vs. NBC in Olympic-like events. Kids would watch in slack-jawed awe, as much for the jiggly joggers, short shorts, and paper-thin swimsuits as for the surreal gathering of star power. Telly Savalas puffing a cigarette during an interview! Robert Conrad pitching a hissy fit! Gabe "Mis-tah KOT-TAH!" Kaplan running as fast as his little mustache could carry him!

The stars were obviously aware of the cameras, but weirdly, the competition felt real. Either it was an unguarded glimpse into who the celebs actually were as people, or these guys were much better actors than we thought. Either way, whoever invented this little gem deserves a gold medal.

X-TINCTION RATING: Gone for good.
REPLACED BY: The show resurfaced in 2003 for a two-hour special but featured contestants from only one network, NBC.

Bazooka Joe

FORTUNE cookies and cereal aren't the only foods that come with their own reading material. Thanks to Bazooka Joe, so does gum.

The little pink, tooth-shattering bricks of Bazooka are notoriously hard to chew, so having a nice reading diversion while you work the jaw is not a bad thing. But don't expect Shakespeare. Joe, who wears an eye patch for no discernible reason, travels through time and space with a cast of idiots, delivering groaner punch lines that weren't even funny in 1954 and "fortunes" ("A penny saved makes cents!") that the artist apparently copied off a random bumper sticker.

Joe's eye patch may be odd, but he's got nothin' on his pal Mort, who usually wears a turtleneck pulled up well over his face. He's either a stagecoach robber from the 1800s or, as the *Onion* suggests, horribly disfigured from the mouth down. Hopefully not a gum-related injury.

Some Joe comics are also mini-catalogs. For a small amount of cash and a pile of Bazooka Joe comics, you could buy yourself a perfumed heart necklace. Or you could just get some other toy out of the gumball machine for a few dollars less, and also get some better gum.

X-TINCTION RATING: Still going strong.
FUN FACT: In one comic, Bazooka Joe rides his time-travel skateboard through space so that he can date Cleopatra. No, we don't know what that artist was smoking, either.

Beer Can Collections

WE don't generally save candy bar wrappers or milk cartons, so what in the name of Billy Carter was the appeal of collecting beer cans? Was it the sound: the substantive clink of the metal? Was it the feel: the heft of the older steel containers or the smooth slip of the aluminum ones? Was it the smell: yeast and, sometimes, desperation?

For most of us, it was can collecting's ability to let a kid brush up against adulthood without getting too close, like holding a used shell casing in your hand or peeking at a *Playboy*. A grade-schooler could inhale the beery goodness of a forbidden fruit while reveling in the sheer power of the packaging. There were flattop cans from when Dad was a kid, with rusty tops and triangle-shaped openings. Pull-tab cans, with teardrop tops and discarded metal curls that could slice skin and insert drunken germs in a single, efficient motion. Schmidt's elaborate wildlife scenes. Hamm's keg-shaped can. Weird one-offs like J. R. Ewing's Private Stock. They were twelve-ounce works of pop art that launched a generation of graphic designers—and also budding alcoholics. Mmm . . . art. Hic.

X-TINCTION RATING: Still going strong.

Benji

E VERY generation has a dog hero, but leave it to Generation X to eschew purebreds like Lassie and Rin Tin Tin and fall in love with a mutt. Benji was every kid's dream dog, from his melty chocolate eyes to his constantly wagging tail. In his eponymous 1974 film, the little pup foiled kidnappers, befriended cops, and even opened metal pudding cups.

Once the first Benji movies hit the big screen, every kid in the country wanted a Benji dog—or a Benji lunch box, record, coloring book, or paperback. The accessories were available, but since Benji was a shelter dog, no one knew how to replicate his floppy looks. A TV show tried, though: 1980's *Here's Boomer* took a similar pooch to the small screen for two sad seasons.

Sure, some mocked the five Benji movies for their sheer innocence. The pooch had none of the snarkiness of Snoopy or the slobbering doltishness of Scooby-Doo. But in a world of war and Watergate and R-rated everything, the family-friendly series was an oasis for grateful parents and easily scared kids. And they might not admit it, but even tougher-shelled viewers gave a relieved sniffle when the little mutt saved the day. Man's best friend indeed.

X-TINCTION RATING: Revised and revived.

REPLACED BY: Although no modern movie dog is quite as famous as Benji, from *Beethoven* to *Marley and Me*, Hollywood dogs keep on barking up the right tree. The creator of the Benji movies, Joe Camp, says a new Benji movie is in the works.

Bicentennial Mania

IN 1976, bicentennial mania swept across America like a runaway Freedom Train. The star-spangled fervor was red, white, and blue, of course, but also green, as our parents shelled out plenty of dough to keep up with the Joneses in an escalating display of patriotism and one-upmanship.

People slapped patriotic patterns on mailboxes and fire hydrants and snapped up cheesy tchotchkes, like Liberty Bell ashtrays and ice buckets. For kids, it was an excuse to set off fireworks whenever we wanted and wear Uncle Sam shirts. For manufacturers, it was a license to print money. And nobody took that more literally than the Federal Reserve, churning out $2 bills and commemorative quarters, half-dollars, and dollars by the millions. We had never seen new-and-improved money before, and the cash was almost too cool to spend. Almost.

With that newly minted moola, even we kids bought a bunch of commemorative stuff we didn't need, like the KISS poster that imagined the rock group as the crew in the famous painting *The Spirit of '76*, complete with American flag, snare drum, and Peter Criss wearing a bloody bandage around his cat head. In the end, it was all about the merchandising. God bless America!

X-TINCTION RATING: Gone for good.
REPLACED BY: Nothing yet. But just wait until the tricentennial in 2076.

Big Boy

WOE to any kid with a cowlick, apple cheeks, and a few extra pounds around his middle. Thanks to Big Boy restaurants and their fat little mascot, a chubby young man was destined to be dubbed "Big Boy" for life. Unfair? Probably. Although if you had a glandular condition, sported Ed Grimley hair, and wore a white shirt and checked red suspenders, well, then, you deserved what you got.

The food at Big Boy was as comforting as a mashed-potato bed with a gravy blanket, but the real draw was the mascot. When you were driving around looking for someplace to eat, his plump fiberglass figure drew you in like a siren's song. He looked like he could be the Campbell's Soup Kids' overweight cousin—and he obviously knew his way around a burger and an order of onion rings. The round little guy proudly held the restaurant's signature double-decker burger on a plate over his head, like a corpulent Statue of Liberty. But was he delivering it to a hungry customer or holding it just out of other people's reach so he could eat it himself?

X-TINCTION RATING: Still going strong, kind of. Today the chain has far fewer locations across the country than it did in its heyday. **FUN FACT:** The double-decker hamburger's—and eventually the restaurant's—name was reportedly inspired by a chubby patron of the chain's original location.

Big Families

IN the 1970s, it wasn't uncommon to have a family of seven living next door to a family of eight, with two families of six across the street. Moms were notorious for blurting out all their kids' names before getting to the one they meant ("Maggie-Molly-Erin-Rob-Alison-WHATEVER your name is"), bedrooms were shared, and station wagons were standing-room only.

TV reflected reality: The Bradys had six; the Waltons, seven; and *Eight Was Enough*. Jan Brady was mocked for longing to be an only child, but was what she wanted so bad? Clothes that weren't pre-marinated in Marcia's Love's Baby Soft? Just one day to walk through their Astroturfed backyard without impaling her foot on Bobby's Legos?

But other than numbers, television's big families and the real ones didn't share much in common. On TV, brothers and sisters formed singing groups and acted out Pilgrim plays in the backyard. In actual big families, if you weren't babysitting your younger siblings, you were babysitting the kids of your older siblings. You never got to pick the TV channel, dawdle in the tub, or choose the pizza toppings. But there was always someone up to play Barbies or Connect Four, or to smack the school bully and steal back your lunch. It was a family affair.

X-TINCTION RATING: Revised and revived.

REPLACED BY: Giant clans are less common but still around. Just ask Jon and Kate Gosselin and the Duggar clan.

FUN FACT: *The Brady Bunch* was originally called *The Brady Brood* because some execs worried that movies like *The Wild Bunch* had tainted the word "bunch." Show creator Sherwood Schwartz got them to come around. Awesomely and ironically, a 1979 flick called *The Brood* centered on a group of mutant children.

Big Wheel

I N 1969, Peter Fonda and Dennis Hopper roared across America on low-slung chopper-style motorcycles. That same year, kids of America roared across their playgrounds on the grade-school equivalent: Big Wheels. "Born to Be Wild," meet "Born to Be Mild." Get

yer motor runnin', head out on the driveway.

With their bright primary color schemes and unique asphalt rumble, Big Wheels were as modern as the moon landing. Owners joined up into grade-school gangs, pedaling through the neighborhood as fast as their scrawny legs would go—at least until the giant, rock-embedded tires wore down to nothing, a regular Big Wheel hazard.

You could jump curbs, pop wheelies, or race down a steep driveway. In those carefree helmetless days, Big Wheels were responsible for more scabs than chicken pox, and not one kid cared. With a taste of the *Easy Rider* life so early on, it's a wonder more of us didn't go into motorcycle racing. Or traction.

X-TINCTION RATING: Revised and revived.

REPLACED BY: Original Big Wheel maker Marx Toys merged with competitor Carolina Enterprises in the '70s, then closed in 2001. An Iowa company, Alpha International, got things rolling again a few years later.

FUN FACT: The basic design was bright red, blue, and yellow, but every kid knew someone with a themed version. Some Big Wheels paid tribute to Q*Bert, *CHiPs*, or the Muppets; one came with a toy rifle, and one even spit bubbles.

Blythe Dolls

YOU know those horror movies where demonic dolls terrify their owners? Blythe dolls would have Chucky wetting his pants in five seconds. Talk about the evil eye; Blythe had eight of them.

Kids pulled a string in the back of Blythe's head to change her eyes to one of four different colors. Cool concept, yes? But something in the execution was memorably disturbing.

When the doll was released in 1972, TV ads touted her eye-color choices as "Beautiful Blue, Bouncy Brown, Groovy Green and Pretty Purple." Apparently someone at Kenner possessed the world's weirdest case of color blindness. On dolls we played with, "Bouncy Brown" eyes were the brilliant orange of NBA basketballs. And purple? These were not the wistful lilac eyes of Liz Taylor; instead, they were the bright pink of Liz Taylor's lipstick. Some kids loved having a doll with semipermanent pinkeye; others were unnerved. And while the orange and pink eyes stared straight ahead, the only two normal eye colors, blue and green, were slid way over to the side. Either Blythe was coyly incapable of meeting your gaze, or she was always checking to see if a better owner was sneaking up on her from another angle.

X-TINCTION RATING: Revised and revived.

REPLACED BY: After Blythe failed to catch on in 1972, she lived on only in the dusty backs of closets for thirty years. Then in 2000, photographer Gina Garan published a book of Blythe images, *This Is Blythe*, restarting the craze and jump-starting a whole new generation of adult collectors and fans. Replicas were produced from 2005 to 2008.

Born Free

WHAT is it about lions that made kids sob like crazy people? Whether it was the Christ-like Aslan in *The Lion, the Witch, and the Wardrobe,* or the nearly toothless Major defending *Napoleon and Samantha* from a grizzly bear, lions rode a good PR buzz that hyenas would have paid big bucks for. Realistically, we knew lions would rather digest us than protect us, but in the movies, they were as loyal as Lassie.

No lion movie made kids bawl more than *Born Free,* based on Joy Adamson's book about raising orphaned lioness Elsa from cubhood and then training her to live in the wild again. The scene in the movie where Joy and George Adamson attempt to leave Elsa, and the confused lioness lopes after their Jeep, is a guaranteed sobfest. But there's a happy ending, as Elsa adapts and eventually shows off her three cubs. All hail the queen of the jungle.

X-TINCTION RATING: Revised and revived.

REPLACED BY: A similar story became a hot YouTube video in 2008. Lion lovers rejoiced at the 1969 clip of John Rendall and Ace Bourke reuniting with Christian, a lion they raised from cubhood before releasing. And there's an Elsa connection: Joy Adamson's husband, George, was the one who reintroduced Christian to the wild.

FUN FACT: Then-presidential candidate Barack Obama told *Entertainment Weekly* in 2008 that *Born Free* was one of the first movies he ever saw, and that he still remembered choking up at Elsa's release.

BottleCaps Candy

T was an odd choice, really, to make candy in the shape of bottle caps. Teeth-breaking metal choking hazards? Let's teach kids to put 'em in their mouths!

But someone at Wonka had obviously stumbled upon a batch of sugary chemical combinations that vaguely resembled soda-pop flavors, and BottleCaps was the name they went with. And then again, who would have thought that there would be a call for Wax Lips or Gummi Worms? BottleCaps seems normal by comparison.

Buying a package of BottleCaps eliminated the option paralysis that came with ordering a real soda. Can't decide between grape and orange, cola and root beer? With a package of BottleCaps, you get them all! The prodigal son of the BottleCaps family used to be lemon-lime, but that was about as popular as lemon-lime soda itself. It's since been replaced by cherry, which makes even less sense, since when's the last time you downed a fizzy glass of cherry soda?

X-TINCTION RATING: Still going strong, but they can be hard to find. Check movie theaters and gas stations, or wait for Halloween. Don't look only for the original hot-pink and green pouch— they're easier to find in tube form now.

Bub's Daddy Gum

I N the 1970s, bubble gum broke out of the flat-stick, five-to-a-pack mold and punked out—the candy equivalent of the repressed kid who went off to college, shaved her hair into a Mohawk, and got her first tattoo. Suddenly, there was fat gum! Long, skinny gum! Double-flavored gum! Gum with liquid centers! When gum came home for spring break, we didn't even recognize her.

A prime example of the trend was Bub's Daddy, which operated under one simple principle: If kids liked a slender stick of gum, then they'd go bonkers for a mouth-stuffing mega-stick. So Bub's Daddy crammed the equivalent of a whole pack of gum into one fat, rounded, foot-long chewable cane—what better way to assure Mom that you were only having one piece?

Made by Donruss, who also cranked out baseball cards, Bub's Daddy was dusted in that same might-be-sugar-but-we-wouldn't-swear-to-it white powder that coats sports-card gum. But flavorwise, this taste treat stood head and shoulders above those sad pink slabs. Who's your daddy now?

X-TINCTION RATING: Gone for good.
REPLACED BY: Bub's Daddy was gone by the early 1980s. To recapture the experience, buy twenty of those plump, pink pieces of Super Bubble, which reportedly uses the same recipe, and stuff them all into your mouth at once.

Bugsy Malone

WE'D like to call this meeting of the "What in the World Was the Deal with *Bugsy Malone*?" support group to order. The oddly popular 1976 all-kids movie musical is our generation's Stonehenge. Will it ever make sense? *Bugsy* was part *High School Musical*, part *The Godfather*—and more than a little disconcerting.

Fourteen-year-old Scott Baio played a mini Michael Corleone in a world populated only by kids. The cars were pedal toys, and the guns shot whipped cream. So far, fine. But then it got weird, '70s-style.

The dark and moody flick crawled into creepy territory with Jodie Foster playing a tarted-up chanteuse and pubescent characters spouting Runyonesque dialogue, like "Put your flaps down, tiger, or else you'll take off." And the wackiest part: When the kid actors opened their mouths to sing, out came adult voices.

What *was* this movie? Like how many licks it takes to get to the center of a Tootsie Pop, the world may never know.

X-TINCTION RATING: Gone for good.

REPLACED BY: Gangster movies and musicals still exist, of course, but never the twain shall meet. *Bugsy* didn't exactly inspire a huge wave of weird all-kid gangster musicals. And that's likely for the best.

FUN FACT: British director Alan Parker was later knighted. Probably not for this.

Burger Chef

AST food wasn't always family-friendly. "Have It Your Way"? Have it our way or the highway, kiddo. Tykes who didn't care for mustard or onions on their burgers were expected to suck it up— starving kids in Africa would have given anything to have some raw onion to chew on.

Into that bleak and grease-spattered world stepped Burger Chef, a chain that offered the "works bar," where patrons could gussy up plain burgers with onions, pickles, ketchup, mustard, and the chain's own "scrumptious sauce." Want to deck your burger with a smiley face of ketchup and a teetering ladder of pickle slices? Knock yourself out.

Burger Chef also earned points with kids by inventing the Fun Meal, a concept later borrowed by a certain clown-owned McFranchise. Their own mascots were the portly, bespectacled Burger Chef himself and his freakishly hyperactive . . . son? Life partner? Stunted-growth employee? Irreparably dense young ward? Well, some short guy named Jeff, anyway, possessor of a giant cowlick and prone to shrieking things like "Burger Chef, you're incrediBURGible!" We still miss the franchise, but at least Jeff finally shut up.

X-TINCTION RATING: Gone for good.

REPLACED BY: Although the chain had more than a thousand stores at one point, a 1982 sale of the company meant most became Hardee's restaurants.

FUN FACT: Many former Burger Chef buildings remain recognizable, despite being disguised as other restaurants or drive-thru banks. Check out NotFoolingAnybody.com for photographic evidence.

Calculators

THE earliest handheld calculators weren't exactly pocket-sized, unless your pocket was the size of a shoe box. They looked like *Star Trek* tricorders and should have come with a doctor's phone number to call when you got the inevitable hernia from lugging them around.

But to kids who'd never seen computers except for room-sized ones in sci-fi movies, calculators were a step into that promised future of hovercraft, robot maids, and talking dogs. And yes, our main goal was to use them to cheat in math class. Take-home tests became a dream, as we aced even the gnarliest extra-credit problem without breaking a sweat. Our only obstacle was those three dreaded words: "Show your work."

We couldn't take our calculators to class, of course, but soon science found a way around that, too, by inventing calculator watches. You definitely wanted to cheat off the nerd who was wearing one of these honkers—if the teacher didn't make him go put it in his locker before the test.

When models with graphing functions started appearing in the mid-'80s, teachers not only allowed them in school but forced us to spend six months of our allowance on one for class. The only problem? For many of us with no math aptitude, the crazy buttons looked like Egyptian hieroglyphics. Question: What's seven times twelve times Ra, the sun god? Answer: A whole bunch of unintelligible gibberish and a D in trig.

X-TINCTION RATING: Still going strong, but a heckuva lot smaller and built into everything, including our cell phones.

Candy Cigarettes

YOU'RE sitting around the card table, a *Laverne & Shirley* rerun playing mindlessly in the background. The Crazy Eights bid is to you, and this could be for the whole pile of Necco wafers. How does a cool kid ramp up the drama? You reach for the red-and-white pack of candy cigarettes at your elbow, tap it dramatically, slide out a sugary cylinder, and take a deep, opponent-intimidating, fake lung-polluting drag. Smooooth. Now, seriously, could you have this much fun with a Snickers?

Just as with real smokes, it wasn't the flavor that was addictive. Candy cigs tasted kind of like sweet chalk, but their gimmick was undeniable. Just as kids faced with a toy steering wheel couldn't resist violently jerking it from side-to-side while making "Vroom! Vroom!" noises, no kids with any sticklike food could resist slipping it between their lips and taking soul-satisfying puffs. Candy cigs were more a toy than a candy, and what were toys for if not for preparing for kids for adulthood, with all its vices and virtues? Smoke 'em if ya got 'em.

X-TINCTION RATING: Still going strong.

FUN FACT: Contrary to urban legend, they're not illegal in the United States, although most brands have quietly renamed the treat "Candy Sticks." Check the low-rent bottom shelves of your local gas station.

Casey Kasem on American Top 40

TODAY we can choose from thousands of songs with a click of a mouse, but when we were kids, we let Casey make the call. With his raspy, melodic tones and distinctively measured—and family-friendly—delivery, *American Top 40* host Casey Kasem spoke volumes.

It was appointment radio. We'd clear our preteen schedules, settle in by the stereo with a bag of Bugles, and get our weekly fix of songs, like "I Love Rock N' Roll," "Pass the Dutchie," and "Come On Eileen." But Casey didn't just spin records—he spun yarns. It was as if we were all sitting around a big, cozy fire and listening to Casey tell the stories behind the songs—with guest appearances by Men Without Hats and Quarterflash.

Even pre-relationship grade-schoolers got the poignancy of his heart-tugging "long-distance dedications," usually about a lost love. They all started like they could be a letter to *Penthouse* ("Dear Casey, A few summers ago I moved from Atlanta, Georgia, my lifelong home, to a small town in rural Wisconsin . . .") and ended with something like, "Casey, will you please play '99 Red Balloons'?" He'd close every show with his trademark reminder to "keep your feet on the ground and keep reaching for the stars," and dammit if we didn't try to do just that.

X-TINCTION RATING: Gone for good.

REPLACED BY: Casey also voiced memorable cartoon characters, like *Scooby-Doo*'s Shaggy, which are still all over TV. But his legacy is on the radio. After Casey retired from *AT40*, Shadoe Stevens and then Ryan Seacrest filled his chair, but they never filled his shoes.

FUN FACT: Casey's married to Jean Kasem, better known as dimwitted Loretta Tortelli on *Cheers*.

Charlie's Angels Trading Cards

MOST girls never got into baseball card collecting, but in 1977 and 1978, sports-card maker Topps hit one out of the park. The company issued *Charlie's Angels* photo cards, with each pack including a piece of powdery gum and a coveted sticker. The cards neatly outlined America's fascination with T&A TV. Bikinis! Two-fisted gun grips! Hair as feathery as a down pillow! Faster than you could say "three little girls who went to the police academy," a generation of new collectors was born.

Angels cards were swapped, stored, sorted, and hoarded according to each girl's personal Angelic hierarchy. Farrah Fawcett's Jill and Jaclyn Smith's Kelly were favorites, but cards showing Cheryl Ladd's Kris in a red-sequined circus outfit were pretty hot, too. (Poor Kate Jackson's Sabrina, eternally the Smart Angel, was trading-card Kryptonite.) Even cooler than the cards, though, were the stickers. More than one kid was handed a butter knife and a severe tongue-

lashing and ordered to perform Angelectomies on their bedroom doors.

To try to encourage kids to collect 'em all, Topps printed a group photo of the Angels on the back of the whole set, urging girls to flip the cards over and assemble an enormous puzzle. Actually doing this was about as likely as getting that damn Mousetrap game to actually trap anything, but there was still incentive to keep chucking your allowance after a new pack. By the time replacement angels Tiffany (who?) and Julie (don't know ya!) earned their wings, the TV card fad itself had gone to heaven.

X-TINCTION RATING: Gone for good.

REPLACED BY: Both TV trading cards and *Charlie's Angels* have come in and out of fashion, but nothing beats the originals.

Chitty Chitty Bang Bang

IT was the movie that launched a million nightmares. No, we're not talking about Mariah Carey's *Glitter*. Though it starts out all lollipops and gumdrops, 1968's *Chitty Chitty Bang Bang* takes a sharp right turn into balls-to-the-wall horror—not necessarily the best combination for a nightmare-prone six-year-old who happened to stumble upon this freak show on TV one Saturday afternoon.

The basic plot sounds harmless: Eccentric inventor Dick Van Dyke fixes up an old jalopy, which turns out to be a magic flying car. What fun! Then the Child Catcher (yes, that's his name) arrives, with his greasy, stringy hair; huge nose; Wicked-Witch-of-the-West voice; and horrific singular focus ("There are children here somewhere; I can smell them"). Why, hello, thirty years of therapy! The Child Catcher is Willy Wonka by way of Hannibal Lecter, using candy to lure kids into his cage.

Why did our parents think this was a children's movie? Stephen King's *Christine* was also about a car with a mind of its own, and nobody plops their kids in front of the TV unattended when that's on. Unleashing the Child Catcher into our developing imaginations? What a Chitty thing to do to a kid.

X-TINCTION RATING: Gone for good.

REPLACED BY: Genuinely frightening kids movies rear their horrific heads every few years. Millions of children have been freaked out by flicks like *Lemony Snicket's A Series of Unfortunate Events* and *Something Wicked This Way Comes*.

FUN FACT: *Chitty Chitty Bang Bang* was adapted into a London stage musical in 2002. It hit Broadway in 2005.

Choco'Lite Candy Bar

I T doesn't seem that the package designers for Nestlé's Choco'Lite were trying all that hard. The brown wrapper, with the candy bar's name in fat yellow cartoony lettering, was about as attractive as a 1970s earth-toned kitchen. But all was forgiven when the bar was unwrapped. The chubby chocolate sections, stamped with an arty fan pattern, featured a unique touch. Inside, the bar was dotted with tiny air bubbles, as if someone magically sucked all the crisped rice out of a Nestlé's Crunch bar, leaving only the chocolate behind.

Those bubbles not only gave Choco'Lite its airy, creamy texture but made eaters stop in their tracks and actually look at what they were eating. It was like peering at the excavated side of an archaeological dig.

Choco'Lite was both dense and fluffy, a contradiction in candy. But it never caught on (did would-be buyers think "Lite" meant it was a diet snack?), and Choco'Lite burned out for good.

X-TINCTION RATING: Gone for good.

REPLACED BY: Similar bars include Nestlé's Aero bar, Cadbury's Wispa, and Austria's Milka Luflée. Some U.S. stores specializing in international gifts and snacks carry them.

Choose Your Own Adventure

Y OU'RE an undersea explorer, hunting for the Lost City of Atlantis, and a stream of bubbles catches your eye. If you decide to analyze the bubbles, turn to page 9. If you decide to take depth readings instead, turn to page 14. What do you do? WHAT. DO. YOU. DO?! You join millions of people around the world in fondly remembering the *Choose Your Own Adventure* books, that's what you do.

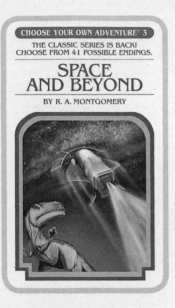

Most books were a pretty passive experience, but this addictive series, introduced in 1980, put kids squarely in the driver's seat. We were the heroes; we got to decide our fates. We'd get to a literary fork in the road and have to decide which way to go. It was an early lesson in how decisions have consequences— even if sometimes those decisions meant we'd get poisoned by a tree frog, gored by a buffalo, or eaten by a dragon.

Sure, in the books you could always backtrack and make a different choice. Not always the case in real life, where one crummy decision often meant twenty years at a dead-end job or a lifetime trapped in a marriage with a guy who never picks his socks up off the floor. Sometimes we would have rather faced the dragon.

X-TINCTION RATING: Revised and revived.

REPLACED BY: After Bantam Books shelved the series in 2003, creator R. A. Montgomery formed his own publishing company and relaunched the books in 2006. In 2010, some of the books were released in an app for iPhone and iPad.

FUN FACT: In 2005, SomethingAwful.com held a contest for fictitious *CYOA* titles. Suggested names included *Choose Your Own Choose Your Own Adventure Adventure, Get Up or Go Back to Bed,* and *Don't Bother, You Die in Most of the Endings Anyway.*

Comic Book Ads

THEY filled up entire pages in Archie and Dennis the Menace comic books. Get a seven-foot Frankenstein's monster for $1! (It was a poster.) One hundred toy soldiers for $1! (They were flat plastic.) Torment your brother with onion gum, 20 cents! (It tasted awful but not a lot like onions.) Learn to throw your voice with a 25-cent booklet! (We ended up throwing the booklet across the room instead.) Try X-ray Specs, a hilarious optical illusion, just a buck! (They made things look kinda fuzzy but never did let you see through that cute girl's sweater.)

Some comic book ads wanted you to sell something—usually greeting cards or *Grit*—in hopes of raking in extra cash. Others just hawked products you had never heard of but suddenly had to have—Sea-Monkeys and Charles Atlas's strength-training program were classics. The ads made at least as strong an impression on a kid's mind as the stories of Archie and Veronica did.

Sure, most kids were smart enough to know that you weren't

going to turn into a muscleman by buying Atlas's thirty-two-page pamphlet, that brine shrimp probably didn't wear crowns and play basketball, and that Mom was so going to ground you if you slipped that fake-blood-producing soap into her sink. But they were so tempting, and if you had a little allowance money and access to a thirteen-cent stamp, well, who didn't send away for one or two? The anticipation of waiting for the mailman alone was worth the buck.

X-TINCTION RATING: Gone for good.
REPLACED BY: Kids' comics today mostly advertise . . . other kids' comics. The goofy gags and products they once hawked can be found at stores like Spencer Gifts, but it's just not the same.

Connect Four

WE were freaks for tic-tac-toe, playing it everywhere—on scrap paper, on chalkboards, on frosty school-bus windows. So in 1974, when Connect Four came along, we immediately recognized it as three-dimensional tic-tac-toe and couldn't get enough. We spent hours dropping checkers into the stand with a satisfying *thwock*, trying to line up four in a row while preventing a pal from doing the same.

Talk about tension. You'd nonchalantly try to distract your friend from figuring out her one remaining block, blabbing about nothing, tapping the checkers on the table, impatiently convinced you were about to slam down Checker #4. Then out of nowhere, she'd swoop in and finish off her own row in a spot you hadn't even seen coming. AAUGH! Damn your powers of misdirection, Jeannine!

It was a feeling perfectly exemplified in the game's infamous commercial, in which bowl-haircutted brother gets beat by his crafty sibling. You remember it. "Here, diagonally!" she crows, as he sinks into defeat and delivers the classic line: "Pret-ty sneak-y, sis."

Thankfully, the game had an ideal built-in way to let off steam: its quick-release latch. The crashing sound of all the checkers hitting the table at once was almost as satisfying as "accidentally" kicking over your sister's Lincoln Log tower. It was as close as kids could come to giving a family member the finger. Pretty sneaky is right.

X-TINCTION RATING: Still going strong.

FUN FACT: In a popular YouTube clip, Kanye West and Jonah Hill play Connect Four to a soundtrack of West's own music. "This is like chess for dumb people," cracks Hill.

"Convoy"

BREAKER one-nine, you got your ears on? Kids had no idea what CB chatter meant, but it sure was fun to pretend, holding a Romper Stomper to your mouth like it was a microphone and blabbing about "putting the hammer down" and "bears in the air."

We discovered the citizen's-band phenomenon when C. W. McCall recorded the 1976 hit "Convoy." You didn't have to understand the exotic new language (what in the world was a "cab-over Pete with a reefer on"?) to immediately fall in love with the romance of the eighteen-wheel lifestyle. "Convoy" told a classic tale of fighting author-ity, with the truckers crashing roadblocks and flaunting toll bridges.

Kids weren't the only ones who loved it. Adults started buying

CBs for their Dodge Darts at such a frantic pace, the FCC doubled the number of available channels. Of course, no one knew any real CB lingo outside of the song lyrics, so real truckers had to suffer through listening to kids, desk jockeys, and housewives calling them "good buddy" until we grew sick of the craze and moved on to the next fad.

Today, the closest kids come to talking to truckers is when they pull an imaginary cord to try and get passing drivers to honk their horns. Still awesome? That's a big 10-4.

X-TINCTION RATING: Gone for good.

REPLACED BY: Cell phones made it much easier—if more dangerous—to communicate while driving, and personal radar detectors help modern drivers stay alert for smokeys.

FUN FACT: C. W. McCall was the creation of a couple of ad guys from Omaha. Bill Fries and Chip Davis (who went on to launch electronic-music group Mannheim Steamroller) concocted the character and named him after *McCall's* magazine. The C. W. stood for country and western.

Crissy Dolls

YOU'D get grounded if you pulled your sister's hair, but Crissy's glossy red tresses were specifically designed to be yanked. Pushing on the doll's stomach freed up her locks so you could then pull them to exorbitant lengths. To shorten the hair, you turned a dial in her back—which was only done for the satisfaction of making it Crystal Gayle length once again.

The first 1969 Crissy doll had the full Cousin It look, with hair going all the way to her feet. Disappointingly, that was later shortened to only hip length, but it was still longer than any little girl's mom would let her grow her own hair.

That was Crissy's charm. Rapunzel hair has always fascinated girls, even if they themselves were sporting the Dorothy Hamill look. Long locks were princessy, they were glamorous, they were . . . a real pain to keep untangled and styled, which is why even those girls who had long hair were generally forced to keep it locked in braids or ponytails.

Eventually, there was a talking Crissy, and there were plenty of accessories, including curlers and ribbons. But most of us didn't care about those extras. All we wanted to do was to grow and regrow her hair, over and over again. The only way you could change Barbie's hair length was with scissors, and that was always a one-way trip.

X-TINCTION RATING: Gone for good.

REPLACED BY: Other dolls have since come out with adjustable-length hair, but Crissy remains the queen.

FUN FACT: Talking Crissy's sayings were unsurprisingly hair-centric and included "Brush my hair, please," "Make my hair short," "Make my hair long," and "Set my hair, please." Kinda demanding, no?

Dapper Dan

IF clothes make the man, then Dapper Dan was a jarring juxtaposition of style over substance, sizzle over steak. Born in the early '70s, Dan taught kids how to buckle, button, tie, and zip, all while indulging his rather, uh, unconventional sense of fashion. From the tip of his yellow vinyl shoes to the top of his caramel-colored head, Dan marched to the beat of his own sartorial drummer.

Dan had his cotton-stuffed finger on the fashion pulse of the '70s. With navy-and-white checked tights, jean shorts, a blue-and-yellow striped shirt, and a bright red vest, his outfit clashed with every possible fabric and color scheme. Dapper? Not so much.

The flamboyant little dude went through numerous looks over the years, including a relatively hip backwards baseball cap and a jaunty canary-yellow vest. Still, he'll always be remembered as the little doll who could zip, buckle, and snap with the best of them, but who had no idea at all how to dress.

X-TINCTION RATING: Revised and revived.
REPLACED BY: Playskool keeps changing the little guy's outfit. He's currently wearing a jean jacket, an orange sweatshirt, and striped shorts.

FUN FACT: A similarly themed Learn to Dress Elmo arrived on the scene a few years later, which was interesting, since Elmo rarely wears pants.

Dark Shadows

SOAP operas, with their mushy, complicated relationships, don't normally offer a lot to hold kids' interest. But the star of *Dark Shadows* wasn't a hunky doctor or gorgeous model; instead, he was a 175-year-old vampire named Barnabas Collins. Anything Luke and Laura could do, he could do better, and with bite.

Forget paternity tests and secret identical twins. Your average *Dark Shadows* episode was a full-on Gothic romp of chained coffins, governesses in nightgowns, creepy portraits, crashing waves, foggy cliffs, time travel, and a lot of scenes shot in the Collins family crypt.

Dark Shadows originally ran from 1966 to 1971, but many kids saw it in reruns years later. A late-afternoon time slot meant plenty of home-from-school kids tuned in with their housewife moms. Tacit parental approval doesn't mean there weren't chilling scenes— Barnabas's little sister, Sarah, made a super-creepy ghost girl, and Angelique, the witch who caused Barnabas's vampirism, had the scariest laugh outside of the Joker. Had *Twilight*'s brooding teen vamps shown up at Collinwood, the *Dark Shadows* coven would have scared the sparkles right off their pasty little hides.

X-TINCTION RATING: Revised and revived.
REPLACED BY: Like Barnabas, *Dark Shadows* will never die. It's

spawned books, two board games, a short-lived TV remake, and now a feature film directed by Tim Burton and starring longtime Barnabas fan Johnny Depp.

Dawn Dolls

D AWN dolls were about half the size of Barbie, and the originals were made only from 1970 to 1973, but their tiny feet left footprints on many a '70s girl's heart.

Sure, Barbie was great, but like your gym teacher, she was large and rather inflexible. Dawn dolls were terrifically bendy, fit easily in a purse or pencil box, and, best of all, made perfect equestrians for a girl's collection of Breyer horses. Barbie would have squashed them.

Barbie's look changed about once every three minutes, but since Dawn had such a short life span, she stayed forever frozen at the tail end of the go-go era. It was hard to even picture Dawn in jeans or pantsuits; she was a minidress kind of a gal from day one. Austin Powers might have tried to fool around with Barbie, but he'd have moved in with Dawn. Shagadelic, bay-bee!

X-TINCTION RATING: Gone for good.

REPLACED BY: Dawn dolls attempted a comeback in the 1990s but just didn't have the staying power of modern lines, such as Bratz.

Debbie Gibson

THEY were the Biggie and Tupac of late-'80s bubble-gum pop, if those rappers had carried lip gloss instead of Glocks. Archrivals Tiffany and Debbie Gibson battled it out— both on the record charts and in the pages of *Teen Beat*—for pop-princess supremacy. Who eventually prevailed? Tiffany had the red hair, tough-grrrl attitude, and jean jacket, but it was Gibson's girl-next-door image, confidence, and—yes, we'll say it—talent that sent her over the top. The string of blockbuster hits, like "Lost in Your Eyes," "Shake Your Love," "Electric Youth," and "Only in My Dreams," didn't hurt either.

Even if you didn't own a Debbie Gibson album, you couldn't escape her reach—high-school hallways were crammed with kids who shared her fashion sense, such as it was. From bowler hats to vests, giant shoulder pads to Shaker sweaters, and skirts over shorts, Gibsonmania rippled through '80s pop culture. Thanks for that, Debbie. There was even an Electric Youth perfume. Because who doesn't want to smell like they just spent two hours sweating under hot stage lights?

Debbie later shifted to Broadway, where she scored roles in *Grease*, *Beauty and the Beast*, and *Les Misérables*. She eventually started going by Deborah (and appeared in *Playboy* in 2005) in a move toward shedding her teen-idol image. But she'll always be Debbie to us, even as she heads into Electric Middle Age.

X-TINCTION RATING: Still going strong. She has acted in such cinematic classics as *Mega Shark vs. Giant Octopus*, with Lorenzo Lamas (*Entertainment Weekly* named it the worst DVD of 2009), and starred two years later with rival Tiffany and former Monkee Micky Dolenz in the even more awesome *Mega Python vs. Gatoroid*.

FUN FACT: Gibson is in the *Guinness Book of World Records* as the youngest person to write, produce, and perform a number one single, "Foolish Beat."

Décor Mistakes

SOMEWHERE around the 1970s, everyone in the country went blind at the same time. It's the only way to explain our parents' sudden lust for the hideous hues and patterns that somehow found their way into our homes. Avocado stoves! Dark brown refrigerators! Harvest gold sinks! All of the previously neglected colors that were rejected by the rainbow lined up and demanded we welcome them into our lives. It may have been called avocado green, but we kids knew the color of boogers when we saw it.

Textures demanded their due, too. Kids hated shag carpeting because Lincoln Logs wouldn't stand up on it, and it ate doll shoes. Fuzzy flocked wallpaper stained easily and made no sense—were we supposed to pet it? Popcorn ceilings, faux-wood paneling, random mirrored walls—if some decorator could think of it, our parents bought into it.

Maybe it was an extension of the free love of the 1960s. Why commit to one style when you could embrace them all? A Spanish mural here, some foil wallpaper there, a little bead curtain hanging here. It was like a conquistador went to a bordello to meet Shaft.

X-TINCTION RATING: Revised and revived.

REPLACED BY: The specific '70s fads have gone quiet, but bad décor lives on. Brocade drapes, overstuffed leather furniture, hunter green—will you be the shag carpet and wood paneling of our kids' memories?

Dixie Riddle Cups

HOW do you know the elephant's been in the refrigerator? The footprints in the butter, of course. Where do cows go Saturday nights? To the mooo-vies.

Corny? As Kansas in August. The knee slappers on Dixie Riddle Cups may have been lame, but they're the reason we all know that when you tell a mirror a joke, it cracks up—and the best way to talk to a monster is . . . long-distance.

Sometimes Riddle Cups would show up in kitchens, where kids would have to fill up about a dozen of the thimble-sized buggers to wet their whistles. Mostly, though, they were staples in bathrooms across the country. We were supposed to use one of the tiny cups each time we brushed, but we'd often yank them all from the dispenser, quickly digest the comedy, then stack them back inside, blissfully anticipating the really awesome riddle that would pop up later.

At the peak of the cups' popularity, in the '70s, Dixie expanded the line to include Dixie Riddle Plates and Bowls. Mmm—dinner and a show.

X-TINCTION RATING: Revised and revived.
REPLACED BY: The cups went to the big wastebasket in the sky in 1977. In the mid-'90s, Dixie reintroduced the concept, inviting kids to submit new riddles.

Dr. Demento

WHAT kid didn't love novelty and comedy songs? When a radio station would sneak "Purple People Eater" or "The Streak" onto the air, it was like discovering Mom had slipped a Snickers into your lunch box. How fabulous, then, to stumble across *The Dr. Demento Show*, a full two-hour Sunday night radio romp, where goofy led into ridiculous led into somewhat risqué followed by just plain silly.

The gentle-voiced Deeeeeee-mento (real name: Barret Hansen) was the lunatic running the musical asylum, honking horns and holding court with a pile of wacky sound effects. There was probably a rubber chicken in there somewhere. But there was method to his madness—he organized songs by themes, featured witty guests, and wound up each show with the most-requested tunes.

The crazy songs he played wriggled their way into our memories. Who could struggle through a miserable week at summer camp without muttering "Hello Muddah, Hello Faddah"? And how daring did it feel to almost swear by singing "I stepped in a big pile of . . . shhhhh . . . aving cream"? Dr. Demento was a teacher, too, introducing us to legends like Tom Lehrer and Stan Freberg and, most notably, to a young fan of his with giant glasses and curly hair who became "Weird Al" Yankovic, undisputed king of modern parody tunes.

X-TINCTION RATING: Still going strong, only not on the radio. Demento's syndicated show dropped off the airwaves in 2010, but he still streams episodes onto his website.

FUN FACT: The doctor reportedly received his nickname after playing the bloody "Transfusion" by Nervous Norvus, leading a listener to comment, "You've got to be demented to play that."

Drive-in Movies

SHOW of hands, please: Whose parents smuggled them into a drive-in movie by hiding them in the backseat of the car to avoid paying a measly $1.25 for a child ticket? Everybody's? That's what we thought.

Drive-in movies were more than just another entertainment option—they were an endurance test. If your parents opted for a triple feature, they'd show up before dusk, jockey for a good parking spot, then drive home bleary-eyed six hours later. In between, it was a mélange of popcorn, bug spray, cigarettes, and beer. Dad would roll down the window halfway and affix the clunky corded speaker, and the tinny audio would pierce your eardrums.

Car after car would be crammed with toddlers in footie pajamas, all struggling to make it through even the first hour of *Freaky Friday*. They'd inevitably conk out in the backseat, only to wake up for a second, catch a glimpse of Mom and Dad making out, and pray for the sweet release of sleep.

Older kids would be out prowling the grounds. Theater playgrounds let you meet and mingle with the tough kids from the grade school on the other side of the tracks. You could slink around and hunt for cars with steamed-up windows, then jump up and terrify the hormone-raging teens inside. By the time you got back to your own Country Squire, who cared if you even saw the movie?

X-TINCTION RATING: Gone for good—almost. There were close to five thousand drive-ins in the 1950s, and now that number is down to only a few hundred.

REPLACED BY: VCRs and cable TV started the drive-in decline. Now giant TVs are making it much easier for the average Joe to approximate the drive-in feel at home.

Dungeons & Dragons

IF you have a twenty-sided die in your junk drawer, a ream of graph paper in your closet, and a tingle of remorse that you never made it past fifth-level elf, you just might be a recovering D&Der. Or maybe you still get together in someone's basement for a Thursday-night game, even though you're pushing forty and have kids and a mortgage and a real job that has very little to do with killing dragons. (We bet it's in computers.)

This fantasy role-playing game first hit the scene in 1974 and trickled down to high-schoolers by the 1980s. This was the hobby for smart kids and misfits, who bonded together over an imagination-bending endeavor that let them pretend they were mighty warriors who didn't get nosebleeds when they talked to girls. It was kind of like a weekly poker game, with Cheetos and Orange Crush instead of cigars and scotch.

Every couple of years, it seemed, parents and principals would cast a magic spell of paranoia and declare that the game was tied to Satanism and the occult. Kids just shrugged it off: They knew they had less to fear from the D&D-playing nerd who sat next to them in English than they did from the roid-raged bully who didn't know an orc from an ogre.

X-TINCTION RATING: Still going strong.
FUN FACT: "Weird Al" Yankovic mentioned D&D in his 2006 smash "White & Nerdy," a parody of rapper Chamillionaire's "Ridin'."

Dynamite Magazine

Highlights was OK for flipping through in the dentist's waiting room, but hipper preteens signed up for *Dynamite* magazine. Sure, you could get it in the mail, but it was supremely cooler to subscribe through the Scholastic Book Club and have your teacher hand it to you in class once a month. School-approved distraction!

Celebs like Shaun Cassidy and Farrah Fawcett decked the covers, but this was no star-crazy *Tiger Beat. Dynamite* had plenty of stand-alone features. A comic strip followed the Dynamite Duo, twins Pam and Bill, who turned into superheroes Dawnstar and Nightglider to solve crimes. Cartoon vampire Count

Morbida offered brainteasers. Magic Wanda taught readers tricks. *Dynamite* even catered to its horse-crazy age group by adopting a colt, Foxy Fiddler, and producing photo-filled features on its growth. The monthly "Bummers" page illustrated kid-submitted gripes ("Don't you hate it when your cat is afraid of mice!") and paid a whopping $5 per selection. Getting one of your "Bummers" published was the grade-school equivalent of having a cartoon bought by the *New Yorker*—instant hallway cred.

Dynamite, and its teen-aimed sibling, *Bananas*, were probably brought down in the end by their own innocence. As kids got more jaded and celebrity culture took over, it didn't seem cool anymore to teach kids card tricks and show them photos of horses. *Dynamite* finally fizzled out in 1992. Talk about a "Bummer."

X-TINCTION RATING: Gone for good.
REPLACED BY: Scholastic still publishes magazines, but no preteen publication has lit a fuse under kids the way *Dynamite* did.

Eight Is Enough

LED by original octo-dad Dick Van Patten and his comb-over hairdo, *Eight Is Enough*, which ran on ABC from 1977 to 1981, was a heaping helping of white-bread wholesomeness.

The Bradfords lived in a Sacramento house that looked normal-sized on the outside but was apparently humongous on the inside, like a clown car. The kids kind of blended together—there was little Nicholas, oldest brother David, curly-haired screwup Tommy, and a bunch of girls somewhere in the middle. Plots mostly centered around benign sibling struggles, like elbowing for time in the bathroom or frantically scrambling to clean up after a party before their parents came home.

Despite the laugh track, the show often dealt with serious topics, too. It had to: Actress Diana Hyland, who played the Bradford mom, died after filming just a few episodes. In the second season, Van Patten's character remarried, bringing stepmom Abby, and a whole new dynamic, into the family.

Eight Is Enough was a sanitized, Hollywood-skewed view of real life, but to us kids, it rang true. Except for the theme song. How many years will it take to finally understand the trippy lyrics, like "A plate of homemade wishes on the kitchen windowsill"? Eighty will never be enough.

X-TINCTION RATING: Gone for good.
REPLACED BY: Reunions. After the show was canceled in 1981, the clan got back together in a pair of late-'80s reunion specials. Betty Buckley was replaced as stepmom Abby first by Bob Newhart's TV wife Mary Frann and then by . . . someone we've never heard of.
FUN FACT: Stepmom Betty Buckley was actually six months younger than Laurie Walters, who played daughter Joannie.

Eight-Tracks

IT'S cool now to mock eight-track tapes as useless doorstops, but that completely overlooks their place in history. Sure, they were bulky, were easily broken, and often made it sound as if both your woofer and your tweeter were under water. But these clunky cartridges arrived on the scene as a welcome bridge to musical freedom. Music lovers who'd once desperately tried to wire their record players into the electrical system of their 1964 Chevy Impala were no longer slaves to the radio and could now play the tunes they wanted whenever they wanted. Well, kind of. You couldn't rewind or fast forward, which meant that once you pressed the button for "The Wreck of the Edmund Fitzgerald," you were committed until the ship sank.

There were other issues, to be sure. The legendary "eight-track click" was a clunky sound that occurred four times during the playing of each tape, sometimes mid-song. You'd be rocking out to the John Denver and the Muppets Christmas tape when suddenly, *click*—it sounded like Kermit had momentarily grabbed Miss Piggy by the throat.

We never understood the magic behind the eight-track. Was it a system of pulleys and gears? Little hippie music gnomes? It didn't matter. It let you play the Carpenters in your car, and that was plenty.

X-TINCTION RATING: Gone for good.

REPLACED BY: Eight-tracks were eventually replaced by cassette tapes, which then succumbed to CDs and MP3s.

The Electric Company

WHEN you'd outgrown *Sesame Street*, you turned on the power with *The Electric Company*, which ran from 1971 to 1977 on PBS. It was entertaining, educational, and more than a little freaky. Who didn't want to punch the kids named Whimper and Whine, for obvious reasons? Ditto for plaid-clad J. Arthur Crank, with his voice set to the annoyance level just below "power drill." And why, oh why, was that giant anthropomorphic lollipop following that poor little girl?

But most of the show was irresistible. We longed to join the singing group the Short Circus, swing on vines with Jennifer of the Jungle, or foil the Spell Binder with Letterman. Some skits were both addictive and crazy-making—the live-action Spidey skits were often the hit of the episode, but it was unnerving that the webslinger had apparently been rendered mute, speaking only through squeaky word balloons.

Later in life, *EC* fans felt as if they'd played minor-league ball with a lineup that went on to become superstars. Morgan Freeman, Bill Cosby, Rita Moreno, Gene Wilder, and Joan Rivers, we knew you when. HEY, YOU GUYS!

X-TINCTION RATING: Revised and revived.
REPLACED BY: A completely new version of *The Electric Company* began airing in 2009.
FUN FACT: The show's soap-opera spoof, "Love of Chair," had a famous catchphrase, "But what about Naomi?" The Naomi who inspired the line was an *Electric Company* producer, Naomi Foner Gyllenhaal, now mom to actors Jake and Maggie.

Encyclopedia Brown

THE Hardy Boys and Nancy Drew had nothing on Encyclopedia Brown, the star of dozens of middle-grade books. Using trivia that was random at best and embarrassingly wrong at worst, Brown solved countless crimes, if you could even call them crimes. Once he figured out that a penny was hidden in a hot dog. Another time he solved the case of a purloined piece of precious toilet paper. All things considered, it's kind of startling that Sherlock Holmes didn't show up and smack the kid in the head with his pipe for daring to call himself a detective in the first place.

But, come on—what kind of crooks flocked to Brown's hometown of Idaville, anyway? It was like the town was perennially hosting a World's Dumbest Criminals convention. How'd you like to live that down in prison: being put away by a ten-year-old who charged 25 cents a day plus expenses? To top it off, many mysteries featured Encyclopedia getting the best of town bully Bugs Meany. (Lesson learned: If you don't want your kid to go into a life of crime, probably don't name him Bugs Meany.)

But the books were addictive. Kids could test their wits against Brown, since each story ended without giving the solution, which was hidden at the back of the book. But since solving the crimes relied on knowing that rotary phones don't have a letter "Z" or that lightning always occurs before thunder, readers sometimes felt cheated. In the most incredibly frustrating solution, Brown found the missing penny by claiming that no one would ever put mustard on top of sauerkraut. So some poor fool was locked up simply because he refused to conform to one kid's rigid view of condiment etiquette? That's grounds for a retrial right there.

X-TINCTION RATING: Still going strong.
FUN FACT: Numerous parodies of the boy detective change his name to the more Internet age–friendly Wikipedia Brown.

Encyclopedias

I'S one of those embarrassing secrets, like wetting your bed: A whole flock of kids were closet encyclopedia readers growing up. Almost everyone's family had a set, and the fact that it might be outdated by a decade or more just added to the frozen-in-amber charm. In the world of the 1962 *World Book*, JFK was forever president and Vietnam just a quaint little Asian country.

Reading encyclopedias for fun was like sitting down with a benevolent but slightly nerdy teacher after class and just letting him ramble. Medieval riddles. Biographies of German sculptors. A full page explaining the history of the letter "Q." A real favorite were the pages on each individual state—how else would you know that Georgia's state bird was the brown thrasher and California's state motto was "Eureka"? Plus, the flipping from article to article and volume to volume prepped kids for a future of channel surfing.

The entire concept of a twenty-six-volume set of encyclopedias seems laughable now. Our parents spent a lot of money for an ungainly stack of heavy books that were outdated from the minute they were printed. But the night before your report on George Washington was due, when the public library was closed and the Internet was just a dream from science fiction, encyclopedias were a gift from the gods.

X-TINCTION RATING: Revised and revived.
REPLACED BY: The general idea lives on online, thanks to Wikipedia and other reference sites.

Evel Knievel Stunt Cycle

ASK any little boy from the '70s, especially those who were partial to rock fights and garter snakes: Dolls weren't exactly cool. Dolls you could try to kill, on the other hand? Totally choice. Modeled after the real-life motorcycle daredevil, the Evel Knievel doll's skeleton was made out of metal—possibly mimicking the makeup of the real-life, much-operated-upon Evel.

First, kids stood the shiny-jumpsuited daredevil on the cycle. Then they frantically wound the handle on the base, and off Evel went, like a red, white, and blue bullet, up a ramp fashioned from a checkerboard and a stack of math books, into the air, and over your sister's doll collection. And the powerful rear wheel kept on spinning, even after man and machine smashed into the wall and ground to a halt, caught up in a tangle of shag carpeting, plastic body parts, and Barbie hair.

Talk about resilience: After a bone-crunching wipeout, sadistic kids could dust off Evel's tiny doppelganger, bend his twisted limbs back into shape, jam him back on the cycle, and force him to do it all again, without so much as a St. Joseph's chewable aspirin to dull the pain. Poor little doll. May he rest in pieces.

X-TINCTION RATING: Revised and revived.

REPLACED BY: In the early 2000s, Cracker Barrel restaurants offered a replica of the 1970s version using the original toy's molds.

The Facts of Life

THE *Facts of Life* theme song urged viewers to "take the good" and "take the bad," and true to form, the show dished up plenty of both. Among the good? Tootie meets Jermaine Jackson. Natalie hires an incompetent Blair for a job at a taco joint. Late-season housemother Beverly Ann has a *Twilight Zone*–style nightmare where the girls are all horribly murdered. (Seriously!)

Among the bad? A first season featuring approximately eighty million classmates, all of whom get two minutes of airtime, even Molly Ringwald. George Clooney's mullet. Annoying Australian Pippa. The random '80s-ness of the musical guests. (El DeBarge? Stacey Q?) The preachy issue-oriented episodes, covering everything from book banning to breast cancer. The groaner punch lines from comic Geri Jewell as Blair's cousin.

But the four main girls had a friendship that felt real, and the fact that dowdy Natalie, for one, didn't exactly fit the Hollywood star mode only lent to the show's charm. And although Mrs. Garrett's advice was corny, she was still a way cooler mom figure than Carol Brady. Still, it was fairly obvious she was running some scam. One wrecked school van does not eight years of indentured servitude make.

X-TINCTION RATING: Gone for good.
REPLACED BY: An embarrassing Thanksgiving reunion special aired in 2001, sans Jo. Seasons of the original show are slowly trickling out on DVD.

Fantasy Island

I T was a remote tropical island rife with magic, danger, time travel, and supernatural intrigue. *Lost*? Nope. Unless *Lost* featured guest stars like Maureen McCormick, Roddy McDowall, and Adrienne Barbeau. And we're pretty sure it didn't.

From 1978 to '84, *Fantasy Island* was a hunk of Aaron Spelling–produced schlocktertainment, led by the smooth-as-rich-Corinthian-leather Ricardo Montalban as Mr. Roarke and Hervé Villechaize as his pint-sized sidekick, Tattoo.

"Smiles, everyone, smiles," the enigmatic Roarke would demand of his bikinied staff as a planeful of new guests disembarked. And who wouldn't smile when they saw the weird mix of B-list celebrities who stepped off de plane? Charo one week, Robert Goulet the next. Bob "Gilligan" Denver, Bill Bixby, even the crying Indian from the don't-litter commercials paid a visit. They were there to get their fantasies fulfilled, and Roarke and his crazy voodoo generally obliged, except for the times when the guests, uh, almost got killed instead.

Mostly, though, the visitors—who seemed oddly unconcerned by running into Don Juan or Frankenstein's monster—would learn a Valuable Lesson, courtesy of mystical Mr. Roarke and his preachy paradise. And that lesson was? If you knew what was good for you, you'd stay the hell off of Fantasy Island.

X-TINCTION RATING: Revised and revived.

REPLACED BY: A 1998 ABC reboot starred Malcolm McDowell as Mr. Roarke.

FUN FACT: When soon-to-be-Mr.-Belvedere Christopher Hewett stepped in to fill Hervé Villechaize's tiny shoes as Roarke's sidekick in the final season, he didn't scamper to the top of the tower to ring the bell every week; he just pressed a button.

Fascination with the 1950s

MAYBE it was because the 1970s themselves were just such an ugly decade, but while they were going on, we kids had 1950s nostalgia jammed in our faces every time we turned around. *Grease* the musical came out in 1971 and became a hit movie in 1978. *Happy Days* started in 1974 and spun off *Laverne & Shirley* in 1976. Retro rockers Sha Na Na were doing the black-leather-jacket-and-gummed-up-hair look even before the 1970s began—they performed at Woodstock, for greaser's sake.

The 1950s we saw on-screen was nothing like the real decade. Fonzie was a little insecure and had trouble saying he was s-s-sorry, but nowhere in his coolness was there a hint of any *Rebel Without a Cause* angst. *Grease* was all about cars and romance and irresistibly catchy songs, and we kids totally missed the bitter edge of Rizzo's "Look at Me, I'm Sandra Dee." (We also didn't get why she was "late." Late for what?) *M*A*S*H* was set during the Korean War, but its sensitive smart-aleck doctors were as '70s as shag carpet.

The '50s revival that we were sold was a manufactured product with any hard edges filed down. But it was sold so well that even our parents, who lived through the real decade, got caught up in it. They weren't all happy days, but a good fantasy will trump reality every time.

X-TINCTION RATING: Gone for good.

REPLACED BY: Hollywood is working on a 1980s revival these days, with everything from old TV series (*The A-Team*) to toys (Stretch Armstrong) being turned into movies. Gag us with a spoon.

FUN FACT: Fonzie's famed leather jacket came late to the show—at first he wore a very uncool green windbreaker. Aaay?

Fashion Plates

TODAY'S kids can watch *Project Runway* and dream of being the next Gianni Versace or Vera Wang. In the 1970s and 1980s, wannabe fashionistas were more hands-on. Tomy Fashion Plates offered a pile of plastic stencils with raised drawings of various heads, bodices, skirts, pants, and shoes. You traced them in the holder provided and decorated your completed creation with colored pencils. The thrill of design without the stabby needles and tangly threads of sewing class!

Fashion Plates separated the Princess Dianas of the world from the Chers. Dianas carefully selected complementary plates, shading them precisely in muted, tasteful hues. Chers thought the whole point was to make an outfit only a blind person would wear. Who wouldn't want to combine a high-necked Gothic bodice with a paisley tennis skirt and roller skates? Pass the purple and orange pencils, please.

A fondly remembered variant, Flip and Fold Fashions skipped the pencils entirely and offered real fabric to wrap around a Barbie-like figure. Tomy also offered the Mighty Men & Monster Maker. Junior Dr. Moreaus could deftly combine a square-jawed blond head and muscle-rippled torso with scaly, reptilian legs and a giant tail. If Superman and a Gila monster ever ended up in the transporter from *The Fly*, this would be the result.

X-TINCTION RATING: Gone for good.

REPLACED BY: There are similar toys today, but the originals are highly coveted for their bell-bottomy charm.

Fisher-Price Little People

THEY weren't cuddly enough to be dolls, or active enough to be action figures. Fisher-Price Little People were representatives from another world, one in which dogs could drive cars, bullies were easily identifiable by their pissed-off perma-expressions, and some tragic communal birth defect meant no one had any arms or legs.

Hourglass-figured Mom always wore blue, her blond hair trussed up as tight as her repressed emotions. Dad and Son shared the same male-pattern

baldness and/or overenthusiastic barber. Sister was straight off the Swiss Miss label, with a lace collar and Heidi-esque braids. But oh, the places they'd go.

The fire station had a bell, a crank-up hook-and-ladder, and a mutant Dalmatian. The garage had an irresistible parking ramp with elevator. The school had a built-in blackboard and changeable clock. But the Little People barn is perhaps the most famous structure—it mooed when its door was opened, and the low dulcet tones just never got old, thrilling kids and sending Mom diving for the Anacin.

Once you'd started a Little People collection, it was easy to integrate your family with other, sometimes competing, creatures. It was not unusual for a household to consist of Fisher-Price Mom, who was married to a Playskool McDonald's crew member, and together they were happily raising *Sesame Street*'s Bert, a smiley blond princess, three mongrel dogs, and an Indian chief in full feather headdress. Even the Bradys' blended bunch was nothing by comparison: "somehow form a family" indeed.

X-TINCTION RATING: Revised and revived.
REPLACED BY: They're still around, but they're now made of pure plastic, not wood, and they're chunkier—and less of a choking hazard.

Flash Gordon

YOU know how when something's so bad, you say it's good? Yeah, *Flash Gordon* isn't that. And yet the 1980 flick, an homage to the comic strip and classic Buster Crabbe serials of the '30s, is so unapologetically silly and entertaining, it wriggled its way into millions of kids' memories like a handful of bore worms. Was it the pulsing score by Queen? (*"Flash, aah-aaaah, savior of the universe!"*) The hammy dialogue? ("I'm not your enemy. Ming is! Let's all team up and fight him.") The scantily dressed—and, due to her thick accent, scantly understood—Princess Aura? Yes, yes, a thousand times yes!

How do you apply contemporary film criticism techniques to a movie that features a flock of hawk-men spelling out words with their bodies? That's an easy one: You don't. While we kids recognized a treasure when we saw one, most adults dismissed *Flash* as a campy lark. Pathetic Earthlings.

X-TINCTION RATING: Gone for good.

REPLACED BY: The movie is available on DVD, and the Sci-Fi Channel tried to revive the concept as a series in 2007, but the attempt was short-lived.

Forever Yours

ARS'S Forever Yours is the only candy bar we know of that successfully went into witness protection. It's still around, but with a different name and wrapper, and even its fans from the 1970s may not recognize it.

Forever Yours was a Milky Way with two differences: The nougat was vanilla-flavored, not chocolate malt–flavored, as with Milky Ways, and the bar was coated in a darker chocolate. And with that name, it made for great romantic gift-giving. Slipping your sweetie a Forever Yours bar delivered an emotional message that just wasn't there if you slapped down a Chunky.

Apparently "Forever" had a limited shelf life—the candy was no longer "Yours," mine, or ours by 1979. But then, a sweet miracle. Mars brought it back—with the exact same recipe—in 1989, first as Milky Way Dark, then Milky Way Midnight. It's safe to assume that many fans of Forever Yours have no idea their old fave has been back for so long. It's a candy Lazarus.

X-TINCTION RATING: Revised and revived.
REPLACED BY: Itself, with a new name.

Freakies Cereal

IF you market it correctly, you could put sugared sawdust in a box, call it "breakfast cereal," and watch it fly off the shelves. Exhibit A? Freakies, made by Ralston Purina in the 1970s, with a short reappearance in 1986.

Freakies looked like Cheerios and kinda tasted like stale Quisp, but that didn't matter. Kids were enraptured by the whole magical world depicted on the box and in memorable commercials. In a cereal-shedding tree lived a friendly gang of seven Freakies, with names ranging from BossMoss to Hamhose to Cowmumble.

Were the Freakies monsters? Aliens? Pencil erasers? It was unclear, but they lived up to the "freak" in their name—BossMoss looked like a clump of broccoli with feet, and the others were so lumpy and melty it was possible the Freakies Tree was located on the banks of Love Canal.

They were ugly, but they sure sang a mean jingle. Sure, it was a little annoying that they rhymed "meal" with "cereal," but who really expects alien monster pencil erasers to understand rhythm and meter? If only Freakies' taste had lived up to their goofy backstory, they might have stuck around longer. As it is, it's a shocker they didn't get their own cartoon.

X-TINCTION RATING: Gone for good.

REPLACED BY: No modern cereal offers the offbeat charm of the Freakies.

Free to Be . . . You and Me

A BOY who loved his doll, a girl getting chomped by tigers, and a dog fixing a sink? Where do we sign up?

A record album, illustrated songbook, and 1974 TV special, triple-threat media powerhouse *Free to Be . . . You and Me* was created when *That Girl* star Marlo Thomas wanted to teach her young niece that it was OK to break gender roles, in careers and life. And looking at today's world, with its stay-at-home dads and doctor moms, there's little doubt that she helped make that happen.

Kids who got this book or album had probably never heard of

women's lib except as a punch line on *Maude*. Many of the major points sailed over our heads; other parts seemed "no-DOY" obvious. No one likes housework. It's all right to cry. Boys can bake cakes, girls can bait hooks, and whatever gender you are, divorce sucks.

But the songs were darn catchy, and the book engrossing, featuring dreamy pencil sketches, snappy cartoons, and one story told in handwritten notes on torn notebook paper. Its most memorable song? "William Wants a Doll," sung by Alan "Hawkeye Pierce" Alda. Its best story? Shel Silverstein's hilarious "Ladies First," in which a demanding little girl is eaten up by tigers.

The book even addressed issues kids didn't know were issues, such as how you shouldn't dress your cat in an apron but should, if he so desires, let your dog be a plumber. *Heather Has Two Mommies* gots nothing on this.

X-TINCTION RATING: Revised and revived.
REPLACED BY: A thirty-fifth anniversary edition of the book came out in 2008. And in fall 2010, Target released a back-to-school ad prominently featuring the "Free to Be . . ." song.

Fruit Brute Cereal

NOTHING says "nutritious breakfast" like a bloodthirsty creature of the night. Or so it must have seemed to the morning-meal wizards at General Mills when they came up with Dracula- and Frankenstein's monster–themed cereals. Count Chocula and Franken Berry made their debut in 1971. Fruit-loving, bow tie–wearing dead person Boo Berry followed a year later. Then, in 1974, cartoon werewolf Fruit Brute bounded onto the scene with frosted fruit-flavored nuggets and vaguely limeish marshmallows.

Today he's nothing more than a pointy-toothed, lycanthropic, and fairly disturbing memory. What happened? The official company line is that the concept simply ran its course. But conspiracy theorists maintain that the hairy, tortured, possibly rabid creature finally found the sweet relief of death. Did King Vitaman and Cap'n Crunch team up to have Fruit Brute whacked? Or is he still out there, baying at the moon, flicking at fleas, and recalling the glory days when the breakfast cereal aisle was an even scarier place to roam?

X-TINCTION RATING: Gone for good.

REPLACED BY: Fruit Brute was felled by the silver bullet of poor sales in 1982, and his successor, Fruity Yummy Mummy, was short-lived. But unholy, undead, and undeniably delicious mascots Count Chocula, Boo Berry, and Franken Berry are all still haunting store shelves.

Funny Face Drink Mix

BACK in 1964, when companies still thought they could knock the morbidly obese pitcher that is Kool-Aid off his pedestal, Pillsbury came out with powdered drink mixes known as Funny Face. Some of the original six flavors were gleefully politically incorrect.

Chinese Cherry and Injun Orange were yanked and quickly reintroduced as Choo-Choo Cherry and Jolly Olly Orange.

Other flavors came later. The delightfully hippieish face of With-It Watermelon, who had sideburns and John Lennon glasses, was later reused for Choco-American soul brother Chug-A-Lug Chocolate. At one point, Tart n' Tangy Lemon was renamed Tart Lil' Imitation Lemonade, in a move that could have only been lawyer mandated.

In the battle of the beverages, Funny Face was almost knocked out early. The drink mix first used calcium cyclamate as a sweetener. When the FDA nixed the controversial ingredient's use in food in 1969, the mix came back fighting with two new formulations, one without sweetener, one with saccharine. Yep, saccharine. Good ol' saccharine! Can't go wrong with— Oh, wait.

X-TINCTION RATING: Gone for good.

REPLACED BY: Pillsbury's stayed out of the powdered drink mix biz ever since, but Funny Face's many premiums, from the ubiquitous plastic mugs to the dolls to the iron-ons, line the shelves of every thrift store in the land.

The Game of Life

LIKE real life, the Game of Life had a mix of fun moments and maybe-we-should-have-played-Atari-instead moments. Its number one lesson? Don't have more kids than you can cram into your overlong 1960s-era convertible. It is also, apparently, a good idea to take the time to go through something called "College," even though the board-game version was fairly deficient in binge drinking, debt acquisition, and drop-adding.

It was unclear who decided to put insurance policies, stock certificates, and promissory notes in a kids' game. Between this and Monopoly, it's like Ferris Bueller's economics teacher was put in charge of kids' game play. Still, few things in Life, and life, were as satisfying as retiring as a doctor to Millionaire Acres while your dopey brother landed in the Poor Farm. Shoulda gone to college, bro.

FUN FACT: One version of the game replaced the cool convertibles with dorky minivans.

Garanimals

I N 1972, kids broke free of the fashion dictator: Mom. Thanks to Garanimals, we could now cobble together a decent ensemble all by ourselves, just by matching the animals on the tags. Even a fashion-ignorant four-year-old could do it. Does this turtleneck go with these plaid pants? Pair up a couple of pandas, and your dressing duty was done: Fashion clash averted.

It was a foolproof system—until you started to experiment. What could possibly go wrong if you paired a monkey with a bear? Plenty. Interspecies mingling doesn't go well in nature (good luck with that relationship, monkey), and it was an even greater disaster in our closets.

Today, though, the simplicity of the idea makes a lot of sense, even for adults. More than one coordination-disabled person, facing a closetful of options, has wished desperately for the good old days, when the only decision necessary was whether to don hippo or zebra.

X-TINCTION RATING: Revised and revived.
REPLACED BY: In 2008, Garanimals staged a comeback at Walmart. The animal icons are a little cuter than their 1970s counterparts—and more active. Now they apparently enjoy playing musical instruments, shopping, and putting on makeup.

Gee, Your Hair Smells Terrific

SHAMPOO really let its hair down in the 1970s and '80s. Body on Tap incorporated beer! Lemon Up had a lemon shaped top! Fabergé Organic wanted its users to tell two friends, and so on, and so on, and so on. But the crowning glory of the shampoo aisle was Gee, Your Hair Smells Terrific.

The name sucked you in. Few products made an entire sentence their name, and such a goofy one to boot. There was no Gee, I Think Your Butt Looks Smaller for jeans, or Gee, Your Breath Doesn't Smell Quite So Rank for mouthwash. The pop-art packaging, with its deep-pink bottle and chubby multicolored letters, further encouraged the purchase. And the scent sealed the deal. It smelled kind of like a combination of your sister's perfume, an opium den, and the hanging air freshener in your older brother's Chevy van. Put together, it smelled of the '70s.

X-TINCTION RATING: Revised and revived.

REPLACED BY: GYHST, as its friends call it, is still made and can be ordered online through the Vermont Country Store. Looks—and smells—just like we remember.

G.I. Joe

EVERYBODY knows G.I. Joe; since invading toyboxes in 1962, the twelve-inch action figure has gained worldwide fame and a foxhole full of military accessories, outfits, and vehicles. But in 1975, toward the end of the Vietnam War, Hasbro relaunched Joe as part of an "Adventure Team" that captured pygmy gorillas, wore pith helmets, and battled aliens instead of acting out scenes from *Apocalypse Now.*

Joe now had a new job and a new look. Some of the changes weren't exactly upgrades: His new fuzzy hairdo and scruffy beard made him seem a little like a plastic middle-school art teacher. His Eagle Eyes, which moved from side to side with a lever on his neck, just made him look shifty. But we all fell for his impressively named Kung Fu Grip, even though all it did was replace his hard-sculpted hands with soft rubber. It didn't exactly give him any martial arts skills, but he could hold things (including hands with another G.I. Joe if he wanted to—nobody asked, nobody told).

X-TINCTION RATING: Revised and revived.

REPLACED BY: The regular-sized Joe got his discharge papers in 1979. Hasbro reintroduced the concept as a 3¾-inch figure in 1982. Hasbro eventually produced more than five hundred different pint-sized counterterrorism heroes and rule-the-world villains, with names like Downtown, Charbroil, and Dr. Mindbender.

FUN FACT: In the 2009 movie *G.I. Joe: The Rise of Cobra*, Marlon Wayans's character comments that another character has a kung fu grip.

Giorgio Beverly Hills Perfume

GIRLS' bathrooms the nation over reeked of two scents in 1982: cigarette smoke and Giorgio Beverly Hills. Just looking at the perfume's name now, decades after its heyday, sets off a massive headache that starts right behind the eyes and soon has your whole head throbbing.

As with Audrey II, the man-eating plant in *Little Shop of Horrors*, the takeover was silent but sudden. One day no one had heard of Giorgio, the next day it had ruthlessly jammed its tendrils into every dressing table and bathroom counter in all fifty states and Canada. Girls who'd been content to spritz on Avon were suddenly pooling their babysitting money and forking over an unheard-of $40-plus for a seductively hourglass-figured bottle of Giorgio. Then there was the decision: to throw away the distinctive yellow-and-white striped box or to keep it, further lording your purchase over your poorer friends.

And once you had the holy grail, there was no sense being judicious about its usage. Other perfumes were for spraying; Giorgio was for *drenching*. The scent reportedly has 450 ingredients, and on a clear day at high school, you could smell every last one of 'em.

X-TINCTION RATING: Still going strong.
REPLACED BY: Giorgio not only lives on but spawned an entire family of descendants, most notably Red in 1989.
FUN FACT: Giorgio's male equivalent was probably Aramis, though Polo and Drakkar Noir also saturated high-school halls in their day.

The Goonies

THIS 1985 flick had everything an '80s kid found totally awesome: bats, water-filled caves, pirate ships, treasure maps, and skeletons with beetles crawling out of their eyes. *The Goonies* even had a little romance, which was, for many of us, the grossest part of the flick. Regardless, it was a two-hour amusement-park ride, and kids in the audience easily imagined themselves as part of the adventure—right along with Martha Plimpton, Corey Feldman, and the kid who played Short Round—swooshing down a water slide, swashbuckling on a pirate ship, or befriending a freakish monster.

Fast-paced and funny, the film was *Indiana Jones* for the middle-school set, introducing a generation of kids to deformed-ogre-with-a-heart-of-gold Sloth, legendary pirate One-Eyed Willy, the toupeed antics of Soprano-to-be Joe Pantoliano, and the Truffle Shuffle—fat kid Chunk's blubber-shaking dance. Most important, though, it

w, Halloween
...d that concept,
...es so small that oxygen mol-
...o squeeze through.

...ny vital bodily function the masks
...ted to let kids see. It was as if the guy in
...ies had never actually met a real child and
...s were the size of BBs. More than one kid stum-

one cre____
night long____
chos passing____

Sparked in ____
1982, authority-figure freak____
old days of biking for miles to u____
parents now instructed us to go only____
then picked through our loot suspiciousl____
homemade popcorn ball looked, Mom w____
it if it wasn't commercially wrapped. Dads____
and police stations, where we joined other def____

proved that underdogs and misfits—the chubby kid, the asthmatic, the brain, the geek—could sometimes save the day, goony or not.

X-TINCTION RATING: Gone for good but available on DVD.
REPLACED BY: There's long been talk of a big-screen remake featuring the original characters' kids. Chunk Jr.!
FUN FACT: Post-*Goonies*, some of the kid actors did pretty well for themselves. Josh Brolin would eventually play George W. Bush in Oliver Stone's *W.* And Sean Astin would grow up—and out—to become a fat Hobbit.

Halloween Candy Paranoia

HALLOWEEN was scary enough to a kid, what with teens out to steal your candy, peeled grapes that felt like eyeballs, and that one creepy neighbor who played the spooky-sound-effects record all night long. But that was nothing compared to tales of real-life psychos passing out poisoned candy and sticking sharp objects into fruit.

Sparked in part by the all-too-real Tylenol tampering deaths in 1982, authority-figure freak-outs slammed the brakes on the good old days of biking for miles to unfamiliar neighborhoods. Instead, parents now instructed us to go only to homes we knew and even then picked through our loot suspiciously. No matter how good that homemade popcorn ball looked, Mom wouldn't even let us sniff it if it wasn't commercially wrapped. Dads drove us to hospitals and police stations, where we joined other deflated kids waiting to get their bags of candy X-rayed. Some super-cruel parents actually put the kibosh on door-to-door trick-or-treating and instead dragged their kids to wimpy parties and malls.

Today, most instances of tampered-with treats have been written off as hoaxes, but the urban legend persists. Hey, son, that Milky Way looks suspicious. Better let me take a couple bites first.

X-TINCTION RATING: Still going strong.

FUN FACT: Poor Charlie Brown is famous for getting nothing but rocks in his trick-or-treat bag, but Bart Simpson may have one-upped him. In one Halloween episode, Bart received nicotine gum. D'oh!

Halloween Costumes with Unbreathable Plastic Masks

I T'S basic physiology: People need to breathe. Somehow, Halloween costume companies of the 1970s didn't comprehend that concept, churning out plastic masks with airholes so small that oxygen molecules had to line up single-file to squeeze through.

Breathing wasn't the only vital bodily function the masks inhibited—they also neglected to let kids see. It was as if the guy in charge of cutting eye holes had never actually met a real child and assumed their eyeballs were the size of BBs. More than one kid stumbled around his neighborhood in an oxygen-starved, half-blind haze, trying to gnaw on a tree he was convinced was a giant Snickers bar. Remove the mask, and the elastic band that held it on would crack like a bullwhip into your face.

Forget today's flammability standards. The pajama-like costumes that accompanied the masks were made of some synthetic material that looked as if it might burst into flames if someone shined a flashlight in a kid's general direction. But the point was pretty much moot in northern climes, where the costumes were hidden by jackets that made kids resemble su-

perheroes with overprotective moms. There's nothing like having to explain to all your neighbors that you were supposed to be the Six Million Dollar Man and not an Eskimo with a bionic eye.

X-TINCTION RATING: Gone for good.

REPLACED BY: Safety concerns have eliminated most over-the-mouth masks. They made a brief comeback in the mid-'90s, when every third kid out trick-or-treating was dressed as the stretched-faced ghoul from *Scream*.

Hal Needham Stunt Set

HOW many kids have you seen playing with a Francis Ford Coppola or Martin Scorsese action figure? None many, that's how many. So why, in 1979, was there a plastic representation of B-movie director Hal Needham, known for directing flicks like *Smokey and the Bandit* and *The Cannonball Run*? The dude had mad falling skillz, that's why. Before stepping behind the camera, Needham had firmly established himself as one of Hollywood's top cowboy stuntmen, so Gabriel Toys released an action figure and movie stunt set, complete with breakaway table and chair, bottles to smash, and a railing for the miniature Hal to crash through.

The coolest part of the set was the catapult designed to propel Needham through the air or jerk him backwards, as if he'd taken a shotgun blast to the chest. The catapult was powerful enough to launch heavier dolls, too, letting budding aerospace engineers fling Barbie or a Weeble into the stratosphere—or at least at the family cat. The cardboard cutout cowboys that populated the saloon were lame, but kids could always set them aside and invite other toys over for a drink with Hal instead. What really happened the night Curious George got goofy on sarsaparilla and smashed Raggedy Andy over the head with a table? They'll never tell. What happens in the toy box stays in the toy box.

X-TINCTION RATING: Gone for good.

REPLACED BY: Nowadays, toy companies are churning out collectible, limited-edition figures of some other fan-favorite directors, including George Lucas, Peter Jackson, and Bryan Singer, although they're not exactly as kid-friendly as Needham's.

Harlem Globetrotters

Larry Bird and Magic Johnson may have inspired a generation to take to the basketball courts, but let's see those guys challenge Meadowlark Lemon and Curly Neal in a pulling-down-the-ref's-pants contest. Winner? Harlem Globetrotters.

The Globetrotters have been around since 1926, blending basketball with goofy shenanigans, acrobatics, and trick shots. But sweet Georgia Brown, it was in the 1970s when they really slam-dunked their way into our childhood memory books. Kids turned out in droves when the Globetrotters mopped the court with the incompetent Washington Generals, showing off their high-flying moves and messing with the half-blind refs.

The Globetrotters starred in multiple TV shows, but none was weirder than 1979's *Super Globetrotters* cartoon. Curly Neal turned into a freak with a giant basketball for a head, Twiggy Sanders transformed into Spaghetti Man, and Sweet Lou Dunbar was able to pull a bomb, a net, or even a couple of chickens from his massive

Afro—all to fight a giant gorilla, a mummy, or a super-villain who stole people's faces. Let's see you do that, Larry Bird.

Then, in 1981, the team cemented its pop-culture cred in the made-for-TV movie *The Harlem Globetrotters on Gilligan's Island*. It's awesome enough that the Globetrotters and Gilligan met at all, but once the Trotters took on a team of hoops-playing robots, you had yourself the makings of a TV classic that was terribly entertaining—and also just plain terrible.

X-TINCTION RATING: Still going strong.
FUN FACT: NBA legend Wilt Chamberlain was a Globetrotter back in 1958.

Hawaiian Punch Commercials

HERE'S yet another lesson TV taught us: If someone asks you, "Hey, how about a nice Hawaiian Punch?" it's a trap. You're very likely not going to get a fruity drink, and in fact, you may get a trip to the hospital thanks to a feisty beverage mascot named Punchy.

Punchy wore a striped shirt, no pants, and a grass hat that looked like he found it in a city dump. The first clue that he had a few anger-management issues? His hand was permanently clenched into a fist. He'd approach a doltish tourist who looked a little like a cartoon Mr. Howell, ask that fateful question, then deliver a fruit-flavored knuckle sandwich to the face. The tourist never learned, and the joke never grew old to kids who had already been long schooled in the Hertz Donut and Slug Bug school of punch-out punch lines.

What the commercials never showed was what happened next. Our guess is that Punchy was eventually booked for battery and sent to mascot prison, along with other commercial troublemakers, like the Cavity Creeps, the Frito Bandito, and the Noid.

X-TINCTION RATING: Revised and revived.

REPLACED BY: Hawaiian Punch added Donny and Marie Osmond as their commercial spokespeople in 1978 ("Go Hawaiian!"), and then Punchy took an extended leave—to serve time?—while the commercials favored shots of bikinied women on sailboats. Today, Punchy's back, and although he hasn't hit anyone in a while, his hand is still clenched into a fist.

FUN FACT: Punchy ran for president in 1992 with the slogan "No one else has the punch." He didn't win.

Honeycomb Hideout

THE world of retro cereal commercials was a strange, often dangerous place. Lucky the leprechaun, the Trix rabbit, and Sonny the Cocoa Puffs cuckoo bird could all starve to death for all the kids in the ads cared. No one was parting with even one teeny marshmallow. It was a world that bordered on breakfast apocalypse.

Perhaps most terrifying were the commercials for Honeycomb. A group of kids met in the Honeycomb Hideout, a simple wooden shack that was sometimes on the ground, sometimes in a tree. Also, they somehow had a robot. But their supposedly pleasant suburb must have bordered Charles Manson's Spahn Ranch. Circus strongmen, Viking berserkers on motorcycles, and, once, Andre the Giant just burst into the Hideout demanding cereal. But they never slaughtered and skinned the kids; instead, they all shared breakfast and everyone was happy. Hopefully one of the kids' dads later came by and fixed the smashed-down door. And moved their family to some safer place, like Beirut.

X-TINCTION RATING: Gone for good.
REPLACED BY: Honeycomb really needs to bring back the Hideout. They crossed into even weirder territory in 1995 with a mascot, Crazy Craving, who appeared to be a big-eyed ball of hair.

Hoopskirts and Camisoles

LOOKING at photos from a 1980s high-school prom, you can't help but wonder: Is this the 1980s or the 1880s? All we know is: Girls' gowns stuck out so far that schools needed bigger gyms. It's like there was a meeting in which Gen X females all came together, burned their older sisters' polyester doubleknit leisure suits, and then settled in for an inspirational double-feature of *Cinderella* and Princess Diana's wedding.

Jessica McClintock and Laura Ashley were among the popular dress brands, but whatever the designer, it was cool to poof the skirt out so far that it had to pay taxes in a neighboring state. Hoopskirts were the choice in the early 1980s, but once a girl experienced the airy thrill of sitting down and having her hoop hula its way up around her eyebrows, she learned of the magic of crinolines. Like hoops, crinolines gave the desired fluff; unlike hoops, when the wearers sat down, they didn't offer up so much of I See London, France, and the North Paris Suburbs.

X-TINCTION RATING: Gone for good.
REPLACED BY: Sexy, sleeveless dresses that reveal more skin than South Beach on a summer Saturday. But the only sure thing in fashion is that each generation will reach back to whatever its parents dismissed as hideously uncool. Like the South, the giant skirt will rise again.
FUN FACT: The best TV scene ever to involve a giant gown was Carol Burnett's "Went with the Wind" sketch. Dressed in Tara's green velvet curtains, with the curtain rod still inside, she drawls to Harvey Korman's Rhett Butler, "I saw it in the window and I just couldn't resist it."

Hostess Choco-Diles and Choco-Bliss

HOSTESS still rules the junk-food galaxy, but some of its lesser-known lights have twinkled out.

What's a Hostess Choco-Dile? They solved the one problem that was preventing Twinkies from reaching perfection—the lack of chocolate. Think Twinkies that were driven through a chocolate-spewing car wash, emerging securely enrobed in a waxy choco coating. Grown-up kids with sugariffic Choco-Dile memories still email and call Hostess, sobbing Choco-Dile tears and begging for their fix. And some are lucky—Choco-Diles still exist, but they're made in only a few West Coast factories.

Sadly, Hostess Choco-Bliss met a sadder fate. It's a shame it's gone because it was a chocoholic's dream. We can only imagine it was introduced at a time when Hostess mistakenly ordered a kajillion tons of extra chocolate and had no idea what to do with it. The resulting treat was a tiny chocolate cake with chocolate frosting on top and layered with fluffy chocolate cream. Even the guy in the commercial went stark raving nutters, shrieking that the treat was "chocolatey, on top of chocolatey, with chocolatey in between!"

But all the repeat use of "chocolatey" in the world couldn't save the Choco-Bliss. Too bad. For chocoholics, even licking Augustus Gloop after his chocolate-river bath couldn't have tasted this good.

X-TINCTION RATING (CHOCO-DILES): Still going strong, but only in some stores on the West Coast. You can also order some from FreshChocodiles.com.

X-TINCTION RATING (CHOCO-BLISS): Gone for good.

REPLACED BY: Recent years have seen the introduction of such limited-edition treats as devil's food Twinkies, banana-filled Twinkies, *Shrek* Twinkies (with scary ogre-green filling), and "purplicious" Wonka Cakes. Thankfully, someone at Hostess is still letting Crazy Cousin Cletus play with the recipe book.

Hugo, Man of a Thousand Faces

P ART Billy Barty, part Lon Chaney Jr., and all creepy, Hugo, Man of a Thousand Faces, has to be one of the single most terrifying toys ever created. Not only was he hairless and wee, but he was literally half a man, with his body ending at the cuff of his oddly dainty blue blouse.

Still, the freaky, follicularly challenged Hugo was good for hours of fun, the male equivalent to the equally unsettling Barbie Styling Head. You could affix any combination of disguises with the provided glue stick—either on Hugo or on yourself. Hugo's arsenal of prosthetics included everything from a nylon wig and glasses to a goatee and fake nose. But they all made him look like a bald, angry puppet wearing a nylon wig, glasses, goatee, and fake nose—and also exactly like James Lipton from *Inside the Actors Studio*.

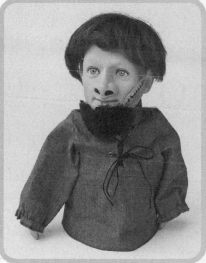

Now-grown kids are still fretting about running into Hugo. Which would be more horrific: waking up in the middle of the night to find the bullet-headed Mini-Me perched on your chest like a cat, or the nightmarish image of Hugo dragging himself across your bedroom floor with his puppet elbows, on his way to the nest he built under your bed? There's no real winner in either of those scenarios, so let's just call it a tie. A horrible, horrible tie.

X-TINCTION RATING: Gone for good. Thank God.
REPLACED BY: Ding dong, he's finally dead. But there is an online "Virtual Hugo," where you can paste electronic wigs and what-not on the freaky puppet without worrying about him trying to grab your throat with his little vinyl hands.

Ice Capades

ONCE figure-skating Olympians have posed for a Wheaties box and put their gold medals on ice, what happens to their careers? From 1940 to 1996, there was the Ice Capades, a glorious and often completely insane bit of frozen kitsch that gave some skaters' careers a second life and gave some kids Technicolor nightmares.

Awe-inducing gold medalists and random community-theater types mixed in a live spectacle that was like a goony 1970s variety show on ice. Skating Ewoks! Clowns riding bikes! The Pink Panther and Snow White on blades! "Hey Kids, Meet the Snorks!" No, thank you. We've met the Snorks, and they don't usually skate. Plus, they're terrible.

The arenas were so arctic, kids would shove the glossy, overpriced programs under their butts so they wouldn't freeze to the bleachers. Millions endured the vaudeville-meets-frozen-water action, all the while hoping a hockey fight would break out between the ice dancers.

The concept hit a new low with a 1989 Ice Capades ABC special hosted by Alyssa Milano and a *Hogan Family*–era Jason Bateman that imagined what would happen if the characters from Nintendo's Super Mario Brothers came to life—and skated. Mr. Belvedere played King Koopa.

Dear YouTube, thank you. Love, everybody—except Jason Bateman and Alyssa Milano.

X-TINCTION RATING: Gone for good.

REPLACED BY: Less lavish and more serious skating exhibitions, like Stars on Ice. Ironically, the growing respectability of ice skating as a sport was more than a little responsible for Ice Capades' demise. People wanted to see Olympians like Scott Hamilton and Dorothy Hamill (a onetime Ice Capades owner) strutting their stuff, but without the guy wearing a Teddy Ruxpin costume.

"I'm a Pepper"

THERE are forgettable commercial jingles, and then there are those that force their way into your brain and sign a thirty-year lease. Few took up residence faster than "I'm a Pepper," the catchy, repetitive, and altogether maddening tune that ran in Dr Pepper commercials from 1977 to '85.

In the ads, actor David Naughton—wearing a white shirt and sweet vest—suddenly broke into song and led a crowd in a musical tribute to the only soda we're aware of that has a medical degree. They may have been Peppers, but they were also nuts. The characters would dive into a choreographed number on the street, on a boat, on a farm, at a wedding, on a mountaintop. An animated Popeye even showed up in one commercial.

"I'm a Pepper, he's a Pepper, she's a Pepper, we're a Pepper. Wouldn't you like to be a Pepper, too?" Definitely. But, for the love of God, only if you stop singing.

X-TINCTION RATING: Revised and revived.

REPLACED BY: In later years, Dr Pepper abandoned the tune for ads featuring Dr. Dre, Dr. J., and "Dr. Love" himself, Gene Simmons of KISS.

FUN FACT: To celebrate the brand's 125th anniversary in 2010, Dr Pepper rolled out original pitchman Naughton to lead a song-and-dance revival of the tune on the floor of the New York Stock Exchange.

In the News

CHOCKA-CHOCKA-BLIPPITY-BLOOPITY-*THWACK!* That's a decent approximation of the futuristic, kinda spooky synthesizer sound that accompanied the spinning *In the News* globe as it announced another of the made-for-kids news segments.

In the News aired on CBS from 1971 to 1985 in between Saturday cartoons and, for some kids, announced the perfect time to take a bathroom break before *The Shazam!/Isis Hour* returned. But for those who stayed, the reasoned and sonorous voice of journalist Christopher Glenn led them through a simple two-minute summary of a major news story. Well, usually a major news story. Once they did a segment on ketchup. But generally, topics were pretty serious—

everything from the fortieth anniversary of the Hiroshima bombing to the hole in the ozone layer to the stampede at a 1979 Who concert.

In the News was written for kids, but it never talked down to them. No euphemisms, no ginned-up happy endings. Glenn sounded like the neighborhood's most reasonable dad, who was neither going to lie to you nor hype things unfairly. And if kids got a little glimpse at the real world to go along with the latest episode of *Far Out Space Nuts*, well, it was like a bite of a crisp apple in the middle of a meal of Ding Dongs: different but not altogether unwelcome.

X-TINCTION RATING: Gone for good.
REPLACED BY: Apparently no one cares anymore if kids are informed. *In the News* is irreplaceable, and Glenn died in 2006.

Iron-Ons and Patches

IRON-ON patches were hard, like a scab, and utilitarian. What kid didn't wipe out on his bike, tear his Toughskins, and beg his mom to affix these poor-man's knee pads? But T-shirt iron-ons were a whole other thing—frivolous, fun, and purely personal.

Kids made pilgrimages to mall stores with names like Shirt Shack, where they thumbed through hundreds of iron-on options. They ranged from 1970s swinger-style disturbing ("I'm warm for your form") to outright lies ("Behind this shirt is a winner") to blunt truths ("I'm with Stupid").

You could also set aside convention and create your own message by invoking the pinnacle of individuality: iron-on letters—some stores had as many as three or four different fonts to choose from! A bored teenage employee would arrange the words on the blank T-shirt, then press them in a giant panini maker. Sure, the little felt letters would eventually peel off, leaving behind an incomplete message, which often spelled trouble. "Keep on Truckin'" was allowed in school. "Keep on uckin'"? Not so much.

And, ah, the odor. We breathed it in. It smelled like burning. And fashion.

X-TINCTION RATING: Revised and revived.
REPLACED BY: Iron-ons and patches just keep on uckin', especially online, with new designs and retro options from the '70s.

Jell-O 1-2-3

JELL-O 1-2-3 involved manipulation similar to a super-complicated science experiment. You had to add boiling water to the fruity powder, put the mix in a blender, add ice water, fill your serving dishes half full, then fill them again. Eventually, magical Jell-O elves broke into your fridge and manually separated the dessert into three layers—regular Jell-O on the bottom, a mousse-like middle layer, and a frothy, foamy top layer.

Digging a spoon through all three layers was like going on an archaeological dig. The lowest level was like regular Jell-O, while level two was thicker, like pudding. But oh, the wonder that was level three. It had the texture of attic insulation and the appearance of an especially cratery part of the moon, but it floated off your tongue and down your throat as smoothly as a toboggan down a hill of fresh snow. Jell-O 1-2-3 was a chemistry experiment gone gloriously right.

X-TINCTION RATING: Gone for good.
REPLACED BY: You can't buy Jell-O 1-2-3 anymore, but you can damn sure make it at home. We recommend the recipe from Carolyn Wyman's *Jell-O: A Biography*. How true it tastes depends on how sharp your memories are of the real thing.

Jem and the Holograms

THERE are many unanswered questions about *Jem and the Holograms*. Did no one ever realize how saccharine and preachy their songs were compared to much catchier tunes by the supposed evil band, the Misfits? (Sample Jem lyric: "Open a book and open up your mind!" Sample Misfits lyric: "Gimme! Gimme! Gimme! I want it!") Were viewers supposed to root for Jerrica and boyfriend Rio when he was pretty much cheating on her with her own secret identity? Did Rio color his hair with grape Kool-Aid? Who had the best name—Kimber, Aja, Pizzazz, or Stormer?

Sure, the show was partially developed by Hasbro to sell toys, but so what? It earned a devoted following that Barbie and the Rockers could only dream of. Who wouldn't want to be a cotton candy–haired rock star by night and an heiress running a girls' foster home by day? Jem was talented, beautiful, and altruistic, but none of it explained why she and her band insisted on wearing eye shadow smeared in weird, tribal patterns across their faces. It was kind of like they wanted to be KISS but didn't actually own a single mirror.

X-TINCTION RATING: Gone for good. Show's over, Synergy.
REPLACED BY: *Hannah Montana* also features a girl with a rock-star secret identity. Now, *that's* truly outrageous.

John Hughes Movies

MAYBE your high school didn't actually look anything like the cushy suburban worlds of John Hughes's movies. But that didn't mean he got things wrong. Sure, we may have never been stuck in Saturday detention with a girl who made art from her dandruff, or given our underwear to a geek. But Hughes set up universes we could all relate to. The villain in your life didn't have to sneer like James Spader. Maybe it was the sour-faced cheerleader in your Spanish class who was never going to drop her grudge. And you might not have had a best friend as cool and yet impressively geeky as Duckie, or as neurotic and moody as Cameron. It didn't matter.

The hearts of Hughes's characters—their loyalty, their wit, and that killer Ferris Bueller ingenuity—these were things we recognized and responded to. Who hasn't felt as forgotten as Samantha in *Sixteen Candles*? Or like the one ragamuffin in a school of Vanderbilts, like Andie in *Pretty in Pink*?

Hughes's movies nailed it: Even the pretty girls and the jocks sometimes slogged through the day as if it were a bowl of wet cereal. The song that rang through the halls of detention in *The Breakfast Club* might as well be every teen's anthem. "Don't you forget about me. Don't, don't, don't, don't."

Hughes's movies didn't, and neither did he.

X-TINCTION RATING: Gone for good.

REPLACED BY: Hughes died far too early, in 2009, at just fifty-nine. He can't be replaced, only imitated.

FUN FACT: Asked by favorite star Molly Ringwald which of his characters he was most like, Hughes said he was a cross between Ferris Bueller and Samantha of *Sixteen Candles*.

Jolt Cola

B EFORE Jolt Cola came out, there seemed to be a gentlemen's agreement that food products would at least pretend to be good for you. But when Jolt poured onto shelves in 1985, all bets were off. It was a coiled snake in a can, packed with almost twice the buzzy goodness of Mountain Dew, the former peak of caffeine-y refreshment.

Even the slogan, "all the sugar and twice the caffeine," just dared you to object. Keep your health drinks, Jolt's ad campaign seemed to say. We'll jack you up like Speedy Gonzales—and you'll like it!

Sure, kids already knew about energy-boosting secrets, like eating a case of Pixy Stix or downing a six-pack of Coke. But it wasn't socially acceptable for minors to intentionally mess with their body chemistry in public until Jolt made it OK. Just strutting around with the lightning bolt–struck can made you look like a rebel.

Jolt was all about the buzz. Although some thought it tasted like carbonated maple syrup, the bite into-a-power-line high kept them coming back for more.

X-TINCTION RATING: Revised and revived. In 2007, Jolt relaunched itself as an energy drink with additions like taurine, guarana, and ginseng. Its manufacturer filed for bankruptcy in 2009, though, so there's no telling how long it'll stick around. You can still find bottles of the original cola in some stores and online.

FUN FACT: Jolt eventually created a minty gum, which packed the caffeine of half a cup of coffee into each piece.

Judy Blume Books

WHEN we had questions about sex, menstruation, masturbation, bodily changes, or just plain growing up, we went straight to our parents or a trusted teacher for straight answers and sensible advice. Right? HA! Instead, we whispered and giggled with our friends, snuck into R-rated movies, and gawked at that copy of *The Joy of Sex* our friend's hippie mom kept in her nightstand.

Thank heaven for Judy Blume. Her books tackled those topics that we were too embarrassed to bring up with anyone, but never did so in an exploitative or lurid way. *Are You There, God? It's Me, Margaret* wasn't just about buying a bra or getting your period; it was about finding out who you are, religiously and otherwise. *Then Again, Maybe I Won't* is remembered as the "wet dream book," but Tony also struggled with the agony of moving, sibling issues, and a friend's shoplifting. And Blume could write for all ages—little kids identified with the hilarious *Tales of a Fourth Grade Nothing*, our moms hid *Wifey* under their mattress, and the much-banned *Forever* was the book someone inevitably stole from a cheerleader and passed around the school bus.

In an era where it felt like grown-ups were still hiding a lot from kids, Blume was the big sister who spelled out the truth. And also taught us that classic playground chant, "We must, we must, we must increase our bust."

X-TINCTION RATING: Still going strong. Judy Blume is still writing, fighting censorship, and also blogging.

FUN FACT: Many a reader of *Are You There, God? It's Me, Margaret* was confused by the mention of belted sanitary napkins, which no longer existed by the time most of us read the book. It wasn't until the late 1990s that the mention was changed to adhesive pads.

Killer Animal Movies

IN the '70s and '80s, our friends the animals turned on us. There was a whole genre of films where anonymous actors were eaten alive by critters that had somehow mutated into killers.

Sometimes the animals were exposed to nuclear waste or experimented on and got huge, like the giant mutant rabbits in *Night of the Lepus* or the creepy-crawlies in *Empire of the Ants*. Occasionally simple electricity ticked them off, like the earthworms in *Squirm*. Sometimes the film just wanted to freak us out about a prediction that had yet to come to pass. We're looking at you, terrifying killer bee hordes in *The Swarm*.

These Mother Nature's revenge flicks were all pretty similar. Lots of spooky music infusing dull setup scenes where characters miss the warning signs that herald the upcoming destruction. Lots of great payoff shots where the audience sees the worms wriggling their way out of the showerhead, or the ants flooding their way up through the sink drain. Gloriously cheapo special effects where normal-sized grasshoppers were made to look as if they towered over cars and homes, or where prop guys tossed stuffed bunnies at actors' jugulars from off-screen. They were no *Jaws*, but they were awesome in their innocence.

X-TINCTION RATING: Still going strong. Disaster movies will always be around in some form. Modern movies featuring killer weather (*The Day After Tomorrow*) or killer Mayan calendars (*2012*) are enough to make you pine for the days of killer stuffed bunnies.

Koogle

E VER since George Washington Carver ground up some goober peas into a paste, kids have been nuts for peanut butter. So is it any wonder that peanut butter jacked up with their favorite candy flavors grabbed children by the throat like crack? Enter the 1970s' answer to Red Bull: Koogle, a jar of sweet, sweet deliciousness that led to an entire generation of vibrating children. Perhaps the googly pair of peepers on the jar and the "Koo-Koo-Koogle with the Koo-Koo-Koogly eyes" jingle were a wink to the wide-eyed crazy gaze of kids hooked on the stuff.

Koogle was simply glorified frosting. And kids knew it. Sure, they may have started with just a taste, maybe on a cracker or a celery stick. But then it got bad, man—real bad—and kids found themselves graduating to an inch-thick slathering between two pieces of bread or two glazed donuts. And when the butter knife clinked against the side of the empty jar, roving gangs of children took to the streets to score some more. Chocolate one day, cinnamon the next. Banana after that. Then probably meth.

X-TINCTION RATING: Gone for good.
REPLACED BY: Nutella, the wildly popular chocolate-flavored hazelnut spread, picked up Koogle's slack. Today, the manufacturer claims that worldwide, Nutella outsells all brands of peanut butter combined.

Kool-Aid Man

HEY, Kool-Aid!" dehydrated kids would yell, and he'd come a-runnin'—a giant anthropomorphic drink pitcher with elephant legs and no pants. Kool-Aid Man would burst through walls, fences, and ceilings with blatant disregard for the damage he left in his fat-bottomed wake. Is there a series of commercials somewhere where he apologizes and sets to work fixing the destruction? Probably not. Hope those kids' parents had Kool-Aid insurance.

When he appeared, boys and girls grabbed and chugged the refreshing sugar water instead of dropping their skateboards and running shrieking to the nearest police station, which is what they should have done. The kids were so thirsty, they never seemed to question exactly where Kool-Aid Man got the drink he was serving up. Our theory: He scooped out some of his liquid insides and poured it into the kids' waiting glasses.

Oh, yeaaah!

X-TINCTION RATING: Still going strong. He eventually got a mouth that moved and—in some commercials—pants.

FUN FACT: Kool-Aid Man even had his own video game, for both Atari and Intellivision. One magazine reportedly dubbed it the "stupidest video game of 1983."

Krackel Bar

LIKE Quisp and Quake, Blair and Jo, or Wite-Out and Liquid Paper, Hershey's Krackel and Nestlé's Crunch candy bars were too similar not to be natural enemies. Both were long, flat bars of milk chocolate studded with crisped rice. Both had names that implied the sounds they made when eaten, if you were eating them in a cartoon. Like the Crips and the Bloods, they even chose opposing colors, with Krackel decking itself out in red and Crunch going for the blue.

Some people think that Pennsylvania-made Krackel is nothing but a poor imitation of Swiss-owned Crunch. Those people are wrong. The original Krackel had crunchier rice, a thinner bar, and a smoother mouth feel, making for an overall superior chocolate experience.

In the 1980s, there were few decadent delights that could compare to snacking simultaneously on a Krackel bar and a cherry Slurpee from 7-Eleven. The Slurpee iced up your mouth, turning your tongue into a little frozen luge runway, and the little sled of chocolate-rice nirvana whizzed right on down. Gold medal to the Americans.

X-TINCTION RATING: Revised and revived.

REPLACED BY: In 2006, the full-sized bar was discontinued, leaving only the squat, chubby miniature Krackels found in bags of Hershey's Miniatures. Krackel may have won the junk-food battle, but it lost the war.

The Krofft Supershow

IN TV land, no one did cheap live-action better than *The Krofft Supershow*, a patchwork of short Saturday-morning segments featuring not-so-special effects and bargain-basement production values. Tying together this cheese buffet were segments starring rock group Kaptain Kool and the Kongs, the non-rockingest rock group who ever rocked. Need proof? The Osmonds wrote their songs.

"Electra Woman and Dyna Girl" used their feminine grrrl power, gigantic video watches, and skintight spandex to battle evildoers. "Dr. Shrinker" and assistant Billy Barty gave kids nightmares by chasing around three teens they'd shrunk to the size of eight-track tapes. "Wonderbug" was a blatant rip-off of cartoon "Speed Buggy," featuring a low-rent Scooby gang who honked a magic horn to transform their dilapidated Schlepcar into a flying dune buggy.

The show was a launching pad for bigger and better acting gigs, perhaps because there weren't many worse ones. Kaptain Kool Michael Lembeck became a regular on *One Day at a Time*. Electra Woman Deidre Hall found fame on *Days of Our Lives*. And "Wonderbug's" John-Anthony Bailey went on to star in adult films. Talk about a magic horn.

X-TINCTION RATING: Gone for good.
REPLACED BY: Today's kids have plenty of weird live-action shows

that probably owe their zany lives to Sid and Marty Krofft. *Yo Gabba Gabba*, anyone?

K-tel

WITH their "it slices, it dices!" rapid-fire carnival-barker narration, K-tel commercials sold music the way door-to-door salesmen once sold appliances. And no wonder, since the company was started by . . . a former door-to-door appliance salesman. Canadian entrepreneur Philip Kives figured out that high-energy TV commercials were a perfect way to pitch records, and sold hundreds of millions of "super hit" compilations with names like *Pure Power*, *Starflight*, *Disco Fire*, and *Street Beat*.

The yell-y, fast-talking narrator hawked hits from Peaches & Herb! Jigsaw! and Molly Hatchet! They were available at Sears! Kmart! and Woolworth's! Once we kids were exposed to the barrage of groovy animation, reverb, song clips, and photos of the bands, we were convinced every collection was a must-buy and begged our parents for a ride to the mall. (Did Stanley Kubrick get the idea for the freaky, fast-cut brainwashing scene in *A Clockwork Orange* from K-tel? Discuss.) It wasn't until we got the album home that the hypnotic spell wore off and we realized we didn't really care for most of the songs, particularly those by England Dan & John Ford Coley.

Too smart to fall for that in-your-face sales pressure? Check your record collection. We'll bet you the latest hit from the DeFranco Family you'll find a K-tel logo or ten.

X-TINCTION RATING: Still going strong.

FUN FACT: K-tel's most popular album was *Hooked on Classics*, which featured catchy classical tunes set to a disco beat and has sold more than 10 million copies.

Laff-A-Lympics

THE 1976 Olympics captured kids' imaginations, and even those of us who knew we'd never be Nadia Comaneci or Bruce Jenner still harbored golden dreams. Animation powerhouse Hanna-Barbera played off our love for the Games with the cartoon *Laff-A-Lympics*, which ran from 1977 to 1979.

Three all-star teams of cartoon characters vied for supremacy: the Scooby Doobies, the Yogi Yahooeys, and the Really Rottens. Despite the fact that the Scooby Doobies had several super-powered heroes, a genie, and a talking car on their team, they didn't always take home the gold. Why the hell not? They should have been wolfing down the competition like it was a bowl of Scooby Snacks. Heck, the Yogi Yahooeys were composed solely of not-exactly-menacing animals, like mice and a duck, and that gigantic idiot Grape Ape. Even the Really Rottens, created to be the Washington Generals of the whole competition, won on occasion—and their team mostly consisted of monsters and hillbillies.

Laff-A-Lympics was remarkably similar to the 1960s cartoon *Wacky Races*, which featured teams of third- and fourth-tier characters (Professor Pat Pending? Lazy Luke? The Slag Brothers?) driving planes, tanks, and automobiles. *Laff* took home the gold, though, not just for bigger cartoon stars but for its stellar host, overexcited pink mountain lion Snagglepuss. Heavens to Murgatroyd!

X-TINCTION RATING: Gone for good.

REPLACED BY: Cartoon races took a backseat to live-action competition shows like *The Amazing Race.*

FUN FACT: The *Laff-A-Lympics* events weren't exactly Olympic caliber. Sports included igloo building, a rickshaw race, and roller skating.

Lawn Darts

THE best childhood toys are the ones with a little element of danger, but this was ridiculous. Lawn darts were a 1970s fixture at backyard barbecues and birthday parties. Why didn't our parents just let us juggle chainsaws or tease rabid wolverines?

Lawn darts looked exactly like the little darts you throw at a tavern dartboard, only they were sized for the Incredible Hulk. Two players would stand at opposite ends of the yard and chuck the darts at plastic rings on the ground, doing a little victory dance when the point landed in the target with a satisfying *snikt*—narrowly missing the kid standing nearby.

There were apparently rules to lawn darts, but who knew what they were? As with horseshoes, we just liked to pick 'em up and fling 'em as far as we could. If we'd just seen the Olympics, we might pretend we were on the United States javelin team. Fans of gladiator movies got to play Spartacus, and girls imagined themselves as Wonder Woman, hefting an enormous spear.

But our fun had an expiration date. In 1988, the Consumer Product Safety Commission banned lawn darts from being sold in the United States, for obvious reasons. Like BB guns, those clacker balls, and that hot melty goop we made monster molds out of, they soon passed into legend, a reminder of the days when fun extracted a painful price.

X-TINCTION RATING: Revised and revived.
REPLACED BY: Fundex reintroduced a much safer version in 2007. Now it's got a bulbous arrow-ish tip that looks like a top, and the dart simply tilts over into the grass when it lands.

Lip Smackers and Lip Lickers Lip Balms

B ONNE Bell Lip Smackers first showed up in 1973 and quickly pushed their way to mouth-moisturizing dominance. Some brilliant marketing mind had the inspired notion to sign deals with soda-pop and candy companies, resulting in such wacky flavors as 7-Up, Tootsie Roll, and Orange Crush. Forget the lip-soothing aspect, these were practically snacks.

Bonne Bell also successfully hawked them as jewelry. Large Lip Smackers came with a plastic hoop on one end and a plasticky rope so that they could be worn around the neck or swung at pesky little brothers.

Competing Lip Lickers by Village Bath seemed to be designed to appeal to the kind of girls who carried *Pride and Prejudice* with them everywhere and thought Gunne Sax dresses were too revealing. They just looked old-fashioned, with their cool little gold metal tins with sliding lids and elaborate designs of fruit and flowers lavished on the tops. You pushed down on the lid until it clicked, then slid it open to reach the gloss. Once you were there, it was almost impossible to resist digging down into the balm and creating a tunnel that went all the way to the bottom of the case.

Thankfully, neither Lip Smackers nor Lip Lickers actually colored your lips. Girls gunked them on so heavily that if they had imparted any color, they all would have looked like recent graduates of Clown College.

X-TINCTION RATING (LIP SMACKERS): Still going strong. Current flavors include s'mores, buttered popcorn, and cookies and cream, and Lip Smackers has also cut deals with Jell-O, M&M's, Kool-Aid, Skittles, and other brands.

X-TINCTION RATING (LIP LICKERS): Gone for good, though other balms use similar sliding tins.

FUN FACT: Lip Smackers was originally designed as an unflavored gloss for outdoor types, until the flavor chemists got ahold of them. Strawberry was the first-ever flavor.

Liquid Paper

PENCILS have erasers, but when schoolkids moved up into the world of ink pens, making a mistake suddenly became as major as chiseling a wrong letter into a block of marble. Options were few: You could scribble out your error and leave an inky mess, or try one of those erasable pens that really just rubbed a hole in the paper.

That's why Liquid Paper suddenly found its way into every kid's schoolbag: Perfection was just a brushstroke away.

Like calculators, Liquid Paper wasn't looked upon kindly by all teachers. Some banned it outright, both for the mess and because we could use it to hide our goofs. Being kids, we didn't just use it to judiciously dab over a typo; we slathered the stuff on like frosting, often impatiently writing on the new surface before it dried. Then we ended up with a mucky combo of gummy white liquid and muddled ink that stood out like bird poop on a newly washed car.

And although the stuff was called "correction fluid," we soon discovered its less-than-correct uses. Some kids sniffed it. And any girl who tells you she never gave herself a math-class manicure with the stuff is lying. Come to think of it, because of the fumes, it's also possible she just forgot.

X-TINCTION RATING: Still going strong.

FUN FACT: It sounds like an urban legend, but it's true: Monkee Mike Nesmith's mom invented Liquid Paper in 1951.

Little House on the Prairie

GIRLS learned a sad lesson about creative license in 1974 when NBC premiered *Little House on the Prairie*. Every girl owned a set of Laura Ingalls Wilder's enormously popular books and eagerly anticipated the frontier family coming to life on-screen.

But then the credits rolled. Melissa Gilbert and Melissa Sue Anderson made an acceptable Laura and Mary, but true fans fell out of their sunbonnets when Michael Landon made an appearance. Landon had a perm, and his face was as clean-shaven as if this prairie Pa had daily access to an electric razor and a can of Barbasol. Every reader knew that Laura's pa had a beard to rival those of ZZ Top. It was as if Abe Lincoln suddenly showed up on the penny with an Afro.

But once kids got over that indignity, *Little House* took off like a team of runaway oxen. Wilder's enchanting characters—stubborn Laura, bossy Mary, and bully Nellie Oleson—shone through on-screen just as vividly as they had on the pages. Viewers even managed to learn a bit about the history of our nation and its frontier spirit. We felt a little guilty complaining about homework after seeing how hard the prairie families fought to establish a one-room schoolhouse, or whining about getting shots after watching Mary go blind from a teenage illness. But then like most shows, *Little House* went Hollywood, leaving Wilder's books behind for more dramatic and unrealistic plots. The nadir was that godawful episode where Sylvia (Who? Exactly!) got raped by a mime.

X-TINCTION RATING: Gone for good.

REPLACED BY: Girls will always read Wilder's books, show or no show, beard or no beard. Everyone has a Nellie Oleson in her life.

FUN FACT: The book's Nellie Oleson was based on three girls from Laura's childhood, including one named Nellie Owens.

The Love Boat

S URE, most kids had no idea who half the passengers on a *Love Boat* episode were. Halston? Elke Sommer? Gloria Vanderbilt? The casting director might as well have just picked random names out of the Beverly Hills Golf Club phone directory. But this Saturday night staple was as warm and soothing as a hot cup of cocoa with marshmallows, especially for kids huddled inside on an icy January night watching the *Pacific Princess* steam into tropical waters.

There were enough familiar faces among the guest stars to make an episode feel like a family reunion (Hi, Morey Amsterdam and Rose Marie! Lookin' good, Annette Funicello!), and even if there weren't, the crew made up for it. It was hard not to love goofy Gopher, although what exactly a "yeoman purser" did was never clear. Julie and Isaac had the coolest jobs on the ship, playing games and making drinks, and Doc was the gentlest of lechers. But Captain Stubing's daughter, Vicki, was the luckiest, as she apparently got to live on the ship and skip school.

X-TINCTION RATING: Gone for good.
REPLACED BY: Robert Urich captained a brief remake, *The Love Boat: The Next Wave*, in the late 1990s.

Love's Baby Soft

EVEN protective moms were OK with their girls wearing Love's Baby Soft. It was practice perfume, smelling a bit like baby powder, a bit like soap, and a lot like what we imagined pink unicorns sunning themselves on rainbows would smell like. It was adulthood in a tiny bottle. Girls bought it at Woolworth's, but they might as well have picked it up on the Champs-Elysées.

The pink round-topped bottles were a fixture on preteen dressing tables, sharing space with Goody hairbrushes, a Tootsie Roll Lip Smacker, and the occasional Breyer horse. Many an impassioned Oscar acceptance speech was delivered into a bottle of Love's, clasped firmly in a twelve-year-old hand. "I'd like to thank the Academy, my parents, and most of all, my costar and husband, Leif Garrett."

Few girls wore Love's Baby Soft for long. Even its most loyal devotees soon discarded it in their rush toward Giorgio Beverly Hills, Poison, or other stinkier scents. But find a bottle today, uncap it, and give it a quick whiff. That's the smell of innocence right there.

X-TINCTION RATING: Revised and revived. It's still around but can be easier to find online than in stores. (Try Sears!)

REPLACED BY: Perfumers are much less afraid to market to preteens these days. There's even a Teletubbies perfume. Good thing Jerry Falwell didn't know about that.

FUN FACT: Other Love's scents included a hard-to-find Rain scent and a snappy fresh citrus scent, Love's Fresh Lemon.

Mad Magazine

N O, kids never really got the appeal of gap-toothed mascot Alfred E. Neuman ("What, me creepy?"), but we couldn't get enough of everything else *Mad* magazine had to offer.

The art was hilarious and often, refreshingly, gross. The barf—and there was a lot of barf—always included a fish skeleton. Who was swallowing a whole fish? No wonder they barfed! The squint-worthy tiny drawings in the margins packed in bonus content where lesser magazines had nothing but white space. *Spy vs. Spy* offered a creative new way to kill someone each issue—from guns and bombs to elaborate booby traps. The fold-ins on the back covers were kid catnip—even the most anti-vandalism among us were compelled to crease the mag to find the hidden joke before we bought it. Too bad we didn't get most of the ones about Nixon, drugs, hippies, or Vietnam.

But the real draw was the spot-on, did-they-really-say-that satire, skewering movies, TV, ads, and life in general. "Nut Court"! "The Crockford Files"! In 1980's "Diff'rent Jokes," "Arnut" tells "Mr. Dumbmon" he's sick of all the short jokes about him and plans to commit suicide—by jumping off a curb.

We were convinced our parents didn't get it. Until we realized that they were reading the exact same magazine—with a lot of the same jokes—twenty-five years before.

FUN FACT: Since it first hit newsstands in 1952, *Mad* has watched as dozens of competitors with names like *Sick*, *Crazy*, and *Whack* ramped up and then faded from view. *Cracked*, with its Alfred E. Neuman-y janitor mascot, held on the longest, from 1958 to 2007, when it moved online.

Malibu Barbie

B ARBIE has been a fashion model, nurse, a doctor, a vet, an astronaut, a rock star, a paleontologist, a chef, an *American Idol* contestant, and a Rockette. But back in the 1970s, Malibu Barbie ruled the beach with nothing more than surfboard-straight blond locks, a sky-blue swimsuit, Jackie O sunglasses, and a Band-Aid-sized beach towel. And, possibly, a precancerous skin condition.

Playing with Malibu Barbie was blessedly simple. Did Mom save one of those little foldy drink umbrellas from her Singapore Sling at Trader Vic's? You had yourself a Barbie beach umbrella. A patterned washcloth made a perfect beach towel.

You could, of course, beg for Barbie's fancy penthouse, but you could more cheaply set up shop in your little brother's sandbox. No Barbie inflato-pool? Fill the Thanksgiving turkey roaster with water and off the high-dive she goes!

Malibu Barbie's biggest problem? Malibu Ken. Lord, what a dork. He sported a molded plastic hairpiece, zero muscle tone, and super-dorky lime swim shorts, which covered some weirdly ambiguous smooth genitalia. Fortunately, Barbie wasn't above dumping Ken and speeding off in her hot pink Corvette with Steve Austin, G.I. Joe, or Major Matt Mason at her side. Once more, unto the beach

X-TINCTION RATING: Revised and revived.

REPLACED BY: In 2002 and 2009, Mattel released Malibu Barbie reproductions. In a nod to her new, more protection-conscious era, the 2002 sun-worshipper came properly armed with a tiny bottle of sunscreen.

Mall Arcades

OUR older siblings had drive-ins and malt shops, but we got our flirt on at mall arcades. The guys camped out at Galaga, Asteroids, or Dragon's Lair, while the girls eyed them from the delicate glow of Miss Pac-Man or Kangaroo. (The weird kids opted for Skee-Ball or the arcade's lone pinball machine.)

It was preteen nirvana: You could hang out with your friends for hours in a darkened room and not have to say a word; jamming a joystick in every direction or slapping at a trackball with both hands was the only communication necessary. And everybody spoke the language: Nerdlish. Most important, the subtle lighting down-played everybody's acne.

The only downside? The high-score credits were unforgiving. One wrong move, and you overshot the swear word you were trying to spell, ending up with "ASD" or "FUJ." Game over, man.

X-TINCTION RATING: Revised and revived.

REPLACED BY: With the advent of cooler home consoles, arcades have waned, and the games are more high-tech and expensive. Now you're more likely to find yourself wearing 3-D glasses and seated in a car-sized copy of the *Millennium Falcon*—and paying $5 for the privilege.

Man from Atlantis

ANY time you visited a public pool, you could tell who watched *Man from Atlantis*. That would be the kid trying his damndest to emulate star Patrick Duffy and swim like a porpoise, bobbing his hips up and down with his arms held close to his sides. More than one Duffy wannabe inhaled a gallon of chlorinated pee-water and sank slowly toward the drain, quickly realizing that the as-seen-on-TV stroke only worked if you were actually from under the sea.

The show ran from 1977 to 1978 and had Duffy playing Mark Harris, a mysterious Atlantean who washed up on shore and was then recruited by a government agency to help fight crime. Like Aquaman, the mermaid from *Splash*, or your average guppy, Harris needed water to survive, which, not surprisingly, became an issue about once an episode. His awesome webbed fingers, tight yellow shorts, and ability to breathe underwater weren't enough to keep viewers interested, though, and *Man from Atlantis* dried up after four TV movies and thirteen regular episodes.

X-TINCTION RATING: Gone for good.
REPLACED BY: Kevin Costner played a *Man from Atlantis*–like fish guy, with webbed feet and gills, in the 1995 big-screen bomb *Waterworld*.
FUN FACT: *Man from Atlantis* was the first American TV series to air in the People's Republic of China. Take that, communism.

Marathon Candy Bar

N 1973, running marathons was not yet as trendy as it would become, but eating Marathons—the thin, braided candy bar from M&M/Mars—ah, that was a different kettle of caramel.

The Marathon bar was simple: caramel just resistant enough to totally mess up your braces, braided and drenched in chocolate. The candy's gimmick was the eight-inch length. It's basic Kid Law: If chocolate is good, more chocolate is better. The bright red package even boasted a measuring stick on the back so kids could make sure Mars wasn't cheaping out. And if your plastic school ruler broke, hey, edible substitute.

Marathon's memorable commercials featured studly Patrick Wayne, son of the Duke, as Marathon John. As Cap'n Crunch had the Soggies, so too Marathon John had his nemesis: Quick Carl, an overcaffeinated nervous wreck who was speedy about everything—

except eating a Marathon bar. Kids, too, couldn't cram a Marathon bar down their gullets quickly. Even a glutton might have to shove half in a pocket for secondary snacking, resulting in more than a few pairs of Toughskins taking a caramel-chocolate bath. Sadly, this Marathon was run into the ground in 1981.

X-TINCTION RATING: Gone for good.

REPLACED BY: Cadbury's Curly Wurly bar, which can be tough to find in the United States, has the same shape and ingredients. Mars has now reused the name Marathon for a Snickers energy bar. Serious snackers are unfooled.

Mattel Electronic Football

TO kids today, the Mattel Electronic Football would feel as primitive as Morse code. But when the handheld device hit stores in 1977, it couldn't have been more addicting if it had been made out of crack with little heroin buttons.

When we scored a touchdown, a little electronic pep band would launch into the doodle-dee-*doot*-do-do "Charge!" song. Kids were instantly transfixed by the moving red dashes and beeps and boops. We would play at the dinner table, in the bedroom, and on the school bus; in class, at choir practice, even in church.

In the game's first edition, passing wasn't allowed, so you'd feverishly tap your thumb on the "forward" button to make your guy run until your knuckles cramped up. Sometimes you'd find a hole and shoot through it, gaining huge yardage. Other times, a wall of defensemen would line up on top of one another, and your only option was to wait until they tackled your little red ass.

Looking back, the best part is that Mattel felt it had to explain what this new phenomenon was—"treat your Electronic Football Game like a calculator"—and even how to hold it. In 1978, Mattel introduced Football II, which included that much-dreamed-about pass function and even let you run backwards. Touchdown, Mattel. Touchdown.

X-TINCTION RATING: Revised and revived.
REPLACED BY: Itself. Mattel rereleased it in 2000.
FUN FACT: The addictive beepy-boopy game eventually got its own iPhone app. Charge!

Maybelline Kissing Potion

THE rollerball goo-delivery system shook up the personal care industry in the 1970s like microwaves shook up kitchens. In addition to Tickle, the ginormous antiperspirant, the new technology was utilized in Maybelline Kissing Potion, clear lip gloss served up in tiny glass bottles. Bubblegum was a perennial favorite, but Strawberry, Cherry Smash, and Orange Squeeze were also popular.

These were for girls who were just too old for Lip Smackers. Kissing Potion was slick enough to look like real makeup and completely impress anyone who was bored enough to search through your purse.

Before the couples' skate at any roller rink, you can bet that half the girls in the place were frantically rolling it on.

But although the word "Kissing" was right in the name, there couldn't have been a lot of smooching going on with this stuff. It was sticky enough to trap flies and made your lips look like you'd just downed a bucket of greasy fried chicken. Mostly, girls too young or too gawky to date rolled it on, licked it off, and rolled it on again. This was why no one bought the Mighty Mint flavor—really, if that's the taste you were looking for, you could just go brush your teeth.

X-TINCTION RATING: Gone for good.

FUN FACT: That's a young Kim Basinger in ads for Kissing Potion.

McDLT

IT was hard not to worship at the altar of fast-food innovation in a decade like the '80s, when corporate America was putting patent scientists to work solving eating problems we didn't even know we had. One troubling crisis was briefly averted by McDonald's with the 1987 introduction of the McDLT.

Who could forget the sandwich's slogan—"Keep the hot side hot and the cool side cool"? In other words, the meat patty was kept apart from the cool elements (lettuce and tomato, aka the "L" and "T"). In *other* other words, you had to assemble your burger yourself.

The McDonald's employee of your choice would serve it up to you in a specially patented and enormously wasteful container with two separate sides, keeping the cool kids on one side of the gym and not letting them mingle with the hot chicks until your car had cruised out of the drive-thru and your friend was taking the corner much too fast, possibly resulting in L and T meeting Floor and Mat.

However, no one seemed to care that both the hot and the cold side sat under the same heat lamp, pretty much rendering the whole two-sides thing a landfill-clogging wash.

X-TINCTION RATING: Gone for good.
REPLACED BY: In America, the last McDLT was snarfed around 1990. McDonald's introduced the Big N' Tasty in 2001, featuring lettuce and tomato, though no double-sided box.

McDonaldland Commercials

I F there's one thing TV taught us, it was that our universe is far from the only one. In some places, crabby green furballs live in trash cans and holler at giant yellow birds; in others, kids adopt friendly sea monsters who come from dysfunctional families. And then there's McDonaldland, where hamburgers are mayors and french fries grow from bushes.

McDonaldland came to life in the chain's commercials starting in 1971, and man, was it a bizarre place. Officer Big Mac was an obviously hapless cop, since his jurisdiction was freely roamed by the shaggy, fry-stealing Fry Guys and the notorious Hamburglar. Really, how hard is it to catch a guy who dresses in black-and-white convict stripes and is always yelling "ROBBLE ROBBLE ROBBLE"? Mayor McCheese wasn't much better, what with his pince-nez spectacles, child-sized top hat, and a Miss America–style sash announcing "MAYOR." What, in case he forgot?

Ronald McDonald was supposedly the star, but everyone's favorite character was the lumbering purple blob that was Grimace. Was he supposed to be a blueberry shake? An endomorphic eggplant? Cookie Monster after a dye job and an eating binge? It seems odd to say this about a place where creatures had hamburgers for heads, but he was by far the weirdest in a weird land.

X-TINCTION RATING: Gone for good.
REPLACED BY: Ronald lives on, but he's not nearly as much fun as a solo act. Bring back Grimace!
FUN FACT: Grimace's awesomely green Uncle O'Grimacey would visit only in March, promoting Shamrock Shakes.

Mego Superheroes

HOLY enduring memories! With their imagination-sparking capes and cowls, Mego Corporation's World's Greatest Superheroes captured a super-powered feeling of glee better than any bunch of toys had before or since. And they were only eight inches high.

The detail was impeccable, from Batman's removable cowl to the Lizard's flexible tail. The female heroes (dubbed "Super Gals") featured outrageously huge hair, although manly men Conan and Thor also sported bouffants that put the Ronettes to shame. The figures had little plastic boots and gloves to lose, and real fabric clothes that you could take off to check out their supermanhood. Obviously, the reason the Incredible Hulk continues to smash everything in sight is that he's still torqued off about the lack of genitalia beneath his torn purple pants.

Play sets and vehicles, like the Batcave (with working Bat Signal!) or the Hulk Van (subtly labeled "Hulk Van"), added an extra level of accessorized fun. But it was just as fulfilling to see what happened when Iron Man met up with the lawn mower, Aquaman fought the crashing surf of a real-life lake, or Robin, the Boy Wonder, was dragged for miles behind a banana-seated bike. What happened? Mom made an emergency trip to JCPenney to pick up another Mego, that's what happened.

X-TINCTION RATING: Gone for good.

REPLACED BY: Mego filed for bankruptcy in 1982 and shut down a year later, leaving a generation of future nerds with nothing more than super-powered memories.

Metal Lunch Boxes

*P**LANET** of the Apes!* Holly Hobbie! *Starsky and Hutch!* When it came to lunch boxes, what was on the outside made what was on the inside taste better. The metal box opened with a satisfying flip of the clip, and you'd slowly lift the lid to unveil your eats for the day, shaking your head sadly at the kid sitting next to you with the wrinkly brown paper bag.

Lunch-box beverages? Less thrilling. Why bring a thermos full of milk from home when you could buy a carton of ice-cold dairy goodness for a nickel? There were always kids whose parents made them, though. They had to sip room-temperature liquid from the

little plastic cup, and their thermoses always smelled like sour cream.

Our theory is that the most popular kids had the most popular lunch-box designs. The kids with Batman or Wonder Woman? Homecoming king and queen. The ones with *The Fall Guy* or Pele? Not so much. And if you were stuck with a nonlicensed design, like plaid, well, then, you were probably eating by yourself anyway.

X-TINCTION RATING: Still going strong, although most are now made of plastic. Many of the metal lunch boxes from our youth are worth big bucks. Kind of makes you wish you took better care of your *Bugaloos* one, doesn't it?

FUN FACT: A Superman lunch box from 1954 sold at auction for a whopping $11,500.

Metal Pudding Containers

YOU *could* lick the aluminum top of a tuna can, but why would you want to? Metal pudding tops, however? Ah, that was a different story. From the late '60s through the mid-'80s, it was practically mandatory to risk bodily injury by running your tongue over the creamy deliciousness that stubbornly clung to the underside of the lid.

Snack Pack, the top dog of no-need-to-refrigerate, portable puddingy goodness, manufactured its last metal cover in 1984, and the addictive opening process is only a gooey memory. Step 1: Insert finger into ring. Step 2: Hold can and pull, listening for the über-satisfying *schlooooosh* of the metal peeling away from its seal. Step 3: Lick the back of the lid. Step 4: Realize that you sliced your tongue on the sharp metal edge, and freak out. Step 5: Keep licking anyway, letting the combination of sweet pudding, cold metal, and warm type O negative trickle across your taste buds.

It was a dangerous dance, but nobody seemed to mind. Kids were heartier stock back then. And so were their pudding containers.

X-TINCTION RATING: Gone for good.
REPLACED BY: Pudding cups now have soft plastic peel-away tops. They do tend to tear when you pull them off, but at least you can lick the underside without needing a transfusion.

MicroMagic Fries and Milk Shakes

I N 1986, once we all had microwaves, along came the reason those appliances were invented—MicroMagic brand foods. At last, a latchkey kid could prepare his own junk food without ever leaving the house, perfect training for eventual grease-spattered employment: "D'ya want fries with that?"

And indeed, the fries were MicroMagic's most fondly remembered offering. These crinkle-cut beauties came in bright-red individual serving boxes, ready to be nuked right in their little cardboard homes. If the finished product tasted a little like the paper they cooked in, hey, small price to pay. The fries were followed quickly by MicroMagic burgers and then, in a head-shaking development, MicroMagic milk shakes.

Wrap your brain around that one. Milk shakes, whose sole purpose in life is to be frosty and icy, somehow achieved that goal by taking a hot dip in an oven. They started out frozen solid, and the microwave melted them just enough to make them stirrable and slurpable. Sure, it felt like Backwards Land, but making a chocolately shake without having to mess up Mom's blender? That's a Backwards Land worth visiting.

X-TINCTION RATING: Gone for good.
REPLACED BY: MicroMagic fries reportedly live on in Japan.

Moon Boots

ASK any kid running around with a bedsheet tied to his neck or a colander on her head: Almost anything can double as a costume. That was definitely the case with Moon Boots, the foamy footwear that stomped their way to popularity in the '70s. They were clunky and puffy at the same time. How is that even possible? Who cares? When you slipped on the boot—a combo of lightweight foam insert, waterproof nylon shell, and massive rubber sole—you were instantly transformed into an astronaut, hopping in pretend slow motion on a backyard moonscape. They'd double as the bottom half of a superhero or KISS costume, and they were also useful for kicking your little brother squarely in the groin.

Grade-school hallways in cold-weather states were filled with dozens of the colorful boots, lined up like slightly effeminate soldiers. Most of us wore department store knockoffs of the Italian originals and paid the price: The foam inserts would turn into mushy sponges if the nylon leaked. Kmart, we have a problem.

X-TINCTION RATING: Still going strong.

FUN FACT: Moon Boots experienced a resurgence after Napoleon Dynamite wore a pair in his 2004 movie. Gosh.

Mouse Trap

MOUSE Trap was supposedly the nation's bestselling game for 1963 and 1964. When '70s-era kids rediscovered it gathering dust in the rec-room closet, most copies of the game had lost their marbles. Also, their plastic divers, bathtubs, bowling balls, swinging boots, and the cages that fell on the probably-also-lost mice. Mouse Trap may have been a board game in the 1960s, but by the time we unearthed it in the 1970s, it was pretty much a puzzle lacking most of its pieces.

Even if you had all the parts, and even if you put them together according to the picture on the box, it was fifty-fifty as to whether the trap would spring correctly. Seriously? If you win in chess, it's not like your queen can get stuck on a square and refuse to checkmate the opposing king. If you win in Monopoly, it's not like the other player's money just refuses to find its way into your account. Kids in 1963 must have been easily entertained.

X-TINCTION RATING: Still going strong.
FUN FACT: An updated version of the game added a toilet.

Mr. Yuk

M WA-HA-HAAAAA! Mis-ter Yuk is mean, Mis-ter Yuk . . . is . . . GREEEEEN." If you saw the 1970s public-service announcement, that eerie refrain likely still haunts you to this day. While psychedelic smoke coiled in the background, the lime-green-and-

black Mr. Yuk made his appearance. Then things really got weird: electrical cords, matches, and bleach bottles apparently all became possessed by the demon from *The Exorcist*, writhing around with murderous intent while a voice taunted, "Home is full of lots of things that children shouldn't touch. Home is full of bad things that can hurt you very much."

Mr. Yuk actually had kids' best interests at heart. The creepy character was developed by the Pittsburgh Poison Center in 1971 and distributed nationwide in the form of stickers parents were supposed to affix to dangerous stuff.

But perhaps the anti-poison contingent did their job a little too well. The PSA was so disturbing, it scared the bejeebers out of every kid with a mouth, making us think that our houses were poison troves, where danger lurked behind every door and bleach, drain cleaner, and laundry detergent were just waiting to leap down our throats the second we dropped our guard.

It kept kids away from poison but left behind a terrible taste in our brains.

X-TINCTION RATING: Still going strong, The Pittsburgh Poison Center still offers free sheets of Mr. Yuk stickers and sells all sorts of Mr. Yuk swag, like pencils, crayons, T-shirts, and wristbands.

Munchos Potato Crisps

IT'S hard to reinvent the potato chip, but damned if Frito-Lay didn't almost manage it with Munchos. The chip started gaining real vending-machine territory in the 1980s. We sought them out because they were bubbly and almost futuristic, nothing like the chips Mom bought. You could almost envision Judy Jetson snacking on these after a tough day at Orbit High School.

If you drew a snack food family tree, Munchos would probably be close cousins of Bugles and vaguely related to Pringles. There may even be some pork rinds in the family. When sucked on, they collapsed inward in your mouth, pulling you into a black hole of salty snack goodness. They seemed to have about the same non-relationship to potatoes that Funyuns have to real onions.

We must have consumed garbage bags full of these things, washing them down with Sharkleberry Fin Kool-Aid while rocking out to Dexy's Midnight Runners and flipping through *Sassy* magazine. They were so '80s, they should have had popped collars.

X-TINCTION RATING: Still going strong. They never went away, just became tough to find. Check dollar stores and outlet groceries.
FUN FACT: Two of Jim Henson's early Muppets appear in an old commercial for Munchos. One's obviously a purple version of Cookie Monster, while the other's a big bald human who sounds just like Kermit the Frog.

Mutual of Omaha's Wild Kingdom

CALL it *Crocodile Hunter*, 1970s–style. *Mutual of Omaha's Wild Kingdom* took families around the globe, as unflappable naturalist Marlin Perkins and his team tried to stuff wriggling anacondas into bags and pull snarling jaguars from rivers. The show was an adrenaline rush for kids, delivering plenty of wildlife action and dramatic music but little blood.

Marlin would introduce segments while wearing a suit, complete with pocket square, and then change into a snappy khaki number when he went into the field. When he got to Africa or South America, Marlin mostly stayed safe in the Jeep, letting sidekick Jim Fowler jump from a helicopter and tackle an elk, or hang from a rope two hundred feet in the air and yank a flailing condor from a rocky crevice. In other words, Marlin was us, and Jim was the equivalent of the little brother we forced to do all our dirty work.

It was death-defying stuff like that that made us kids dig our fingers into the arms of our sofa and count the seconds until the next episode. With its snapping crocodiles, barking sea lions, and hissing water monitor lizards, *Wild Kingdom* always seemed one uncertain second away from turning into *When Animals Attack*.

X-TINCTION RATING: Revised and revived.
REPLACED BY: The original series ran from 1963 to 1985. Animal Planet started producing new episodes in 2002, narrated by Alec Baldwin.
FUN FACT: *Wild Kingdom* sidekick Jim Fowler went on to bring a cavalcade of animals onto *The Tonight Show*, including a kinkajou that spit bananas on Johnny Carson's new sport coat.

Mystery Date

DON'T you hate when this happens? You're wearing a bathing suit when your date shows up and wants to go skiing. Or you're wearing shorts when your sideburned Adonis appears in a purple velvet tuxedo. Or you're all gussied up in an evening gown when a bespectacled Poindexter dubbed the Dud arrives, all set for a date of Heavy Reading or Mainframe Punch-Card Feeding, or whatever nerds did before D&D. Such was life inside Mystery Date, a game that felt delightfully dated even by the time the 1960s version was modernized in 1972.

Players tried to collect the three cards required for each themed date. Apparently without a green-and-white checked hat and knee-socks, you couldn't embark on a successful picnic—who knew? Then

you spun the doorknob in the center of the board and opened it. If your dorky date wasn't prepared for the same enchanted evening, you slammed the door in his face. That'll teach him to pay attention the next time you make plans!

If you found the Dud, you were apparently so traumatized that you also punished yourself by giving up your matched set of cards. Milton Bradley was oblivious to the fact that in just three years, the Dud would found Microsoft and could buy his date enough kneesocks and checked hats to outfit the entire cast of *That Girl*.

X-TINCTION RATING: Revised and revived.

REPLACED BY: The 2006 hit TV movie *High School Musical* spawned its own version of Mystery Date. Girls now prepared for salsa dancing, karaoke, roller skating, or a basketball game, and instead

of the Dud as punishment, homeroom teacher Ms. Darbus handed
out detention.

Nancy Drew

THINGS Nancy Drew didn't have: School. A real job. A curfew.
Things Nancy did have: Her own convertible. A never-ending
stash of money. A boyfriend (Ned Nickerson) and two best girlfriends
(Bess and George). A housekeeper. Name recognition in every police
department in the land.

Thing Nancy had that we never quite understood: Titian hair.
Titian? Hair color aside, Nancy's never-ending series of detective
books helped create a generation of wannabe girl sleuths, not to
mention book collectors.

A new Nancy mystery (ours were the yellow-spined picture covers) came out every few months, and rabid readers bought them all.
They had great titles and even better covers, although *The Crooked
Bannister* should really be renamed *The Sad Robot Made Out of Tinfoil
and Random Car Parts. Oh, and He's Standing Near a Bannister.* But they
all offered a satisfying if not exactly mind-boggling mystery that
wrapped up cleanly in a neat two hundred pages. And the mystery of
titian? Turned out it's pretty much red. Nancy could have told us that.

X-TINCTION RATING: Revised and revived.
REPLACED BY: Nancy's latest series has her driving a hybrid and
using a cell phone.
FUN FACT: Perhaps the weirdest Nancy Drew plot ever occurs in

the revised version of *The Mystery of the Moss-Covered Mansion*. The 1941 original involved wild animals kept in a mysterious house, but the 1971 update has Nancy fighting to prove the innocence of a man who was accused of sending a truck full of explosive oranges into what's now Kennedy Space Center. Talk about getting juiced.

Nerds

WHEN Willy Wonka introduced Nerds in 1983, the new treat hit the playground community with all the force of an F5 tornado. They were candy! But they looked like aquarium rocks! Had a daringly uncool name! Boasted slightly scary handless mascots wearing tennis shoes! Were small enough to sneak into your mouth during math class!

Best of all, Wonka managed to shove two distinctly different flavors into every teeny little divided box. So even if one side was boring (cherry) or nasty (banana), the other side might offer redemption (cherry cola). Nerds helped us realize that not everyone's taste buds were the same, and for good reason. You might haaate the green apple flavor, but your best friend might love it so much she'd be dying to swap you for her blueberry ones.

The product creativity division for Nerds never stopped coming out with cool variations. Hot and Cold Nerds featured spicy cinnamon on one side and the cool relief of wintergreen on the other. Sour Nerds made you pucker like old Grandma Walton. Rainbow Nerds mixed all flavors together.

The 1980s may have been the Decade of Nerds—Bill Gates, the *Revenge of the Nerds* movie, Steve Urkel, everyone Anthony Michael Hall ever played—but none of them were as universally beloved as the candy.

X-TINCTION RATING: Still going strong.
FUN FACT: Short-lived Nerds cereal not only shared the two-flavor, divided-box motif, but let you mail away for a divided bowl with a removable gate that separated the two tastes.

The New Scooby-Doo Movies

EVER have one of those world-mixing dreams, where people you knew from grade school suddenly show up at your workplace and it just seems natural that everyone knows everyone else? Such was the world of *The New Scooby-Doo Movies*, which aired from 1972 to 1973 and eternally ever after in reruns. Each episode featured a truly bizarre real-life or fellow cartoon guest star who just happened to show up to help the gang pull the latest rubber mask off the latest criminal gardener. It was like the All-Star Game of cartoons.

Guests who were already dead in real life? Laurel and Hardy. Guests who just wouldn't go away? The Harlem Globetrotters showed up three times. Most awkward guests? Sonny and Cher were just as mean to each other in cartoon form as they were in real life.

But perhaps no guest put up with more than Mama Cass Elliot, who was the target of fat jokes from Shaggy and was drawn with a double chin and orange-and-magenta muumuu. Zoinks!

X-TINCTION RATING: Gone for good.

REPLACED BY: Scooby-Doo himself will never die, but they really need to bring back the guest star concept. Imagine the awesomeness if Tina Fey, Beyoncé, Whoopi Goldberg, and Peyton Manning showed up to go for a ride in the Mystery Machine.

A Nightmare on Elm Street

O NE, two, Freddy's coming for you. Three, four, better lock your door." Five, six, those were some disturbing flicks. Beginning in 1984, the *Nightmare on Elm Street* movies introduced us to Freddy Krueger, wise-cracking slasher with razor-sharp fingers; a ratty, red-and-green-striped sweater; and a complexion not even Stridex could help.

At least Freddy enjoyed his job. We applauded when he sucked Johnny Depp into his bed and spit him back out as a geyser of future-Oscar-nominee blood. The cheesy one-liners didn't hurt, either. "This is it, Jennifer: Your big break in TV," Freddy sneered, as he smashed a girl's head into a television screen.

Freddy eventually overdid the stand-up and became a cuddly, schlocky parody of his former self, with toys like talking dolls, Matchbox cars, and even a squirt gun in the shape of his hideous head. Why would a kid want to play with a scarred mass murderer? Not exactly family-friendly entertainment. Unless you're part of the Manson family.

X-TINCTION RATING: Revised and revived.

REPLACED BY: Robert Englund starred as Freddy in nine movies, including one where he took on hockey-masked creep Jason. Jackie Earle Haley from *The Bad News Bears* filled the iconic sweater in a 2010 remake.

O'Boisies Potato Chips

OH, Idaho. You and your oh-so-easily mocked state name ("That's right, you da ho") and embarrassing license plate slogan ("Famous Potatoes!"). But your capital city and your famous taters lent themselves to one of our favorite 1980s snack foods, O'Boisies potato chips.

Ever seen a tortilla being made, how the dough blisters and pops on the griddle? That's how O'Boisies looked, slightly resembling photos of the lunar surface, dotted with bubbles on both sides. Some thought the resulting product always tasted stale; others thought the

bubbles held in the salt and that the earthy, potatoey flavor was a plus.

O'Boisies also daringly broke the unwritten consumer flavor-naming code—the "original" flavor, instead of being plain, had a distinct garlic taste, perfect for those days when you were fresh outta dip. And these treats almost single-handedly taught a generation a new word for "noisy," thanks to their commercials featuring the Keebler elves loudly chomping while a jingle bragged "O'Boisies are O'Boisterous!"

X-TINCTION RATING: Revised and revived.

REPLACED BY: O'Boisies were Keebler's top salty snack for a time, but the elves eventually sold out, and O'Boisies vanished in the early 2000s. Thankfully, an Arizona company started remaking them in 2009. The relaunched O'Boisies can be O'Hard to O'Find. As with Munchos, we've had the best luck finding these at dollar stores and outlets.

FUN FACT: The late Miles Willard, an Idaho engineer who helped develop O'Boisies, also developed another crunchy cult favorite, Tato Skins.

The Official Preppy Handbook

WHEN Lisa Birnbach's *Official Preppy Handbook* hit bookstore shelves in 1980, American schools were instantly awash in pastel. Preppy pushed aside hippie, and kids everywhere donned the uniform of the day. It was simple, once you cracked the code. Collar up on your Izod shirt? Check. Sperry Top-Siders on? Gotcha. Argyle underwear? Yes, please.

The look, based on fashion from New England prep schools, poured over middle America like a pretentious tidal wave. It took a lot of the guesswork out of getting dressed, sure, but mostly it helped kids in fly-over country find something in common with their hipper East Coast counterparts. No, there weren't many Muffys or Chips in the Midwest, but wearing a shirt with a little crocodile on it made even Stacys and Scotts feel a little bit snooty.

The book, although satirical, became a bible of sorts for Waspy wannabes, tackling thorny issues ranging from the politics of monogramming to explaining why "summer" is a verb. It didn't take long for preppy-wear like polo shirts and khakis to make it into the mainstream, and stay there. Flip open any J.Crew catalog. Odds are you're wearing the pants on page 27.

X-TINCTION RATING: Still going strong. Lisa Birnbach wrote a long-awaited sequel, *True Prep*, in 2010.

FUN FACT: *National Lampoon* famously parodied Izod's alligator shirt by making one of its own, featuring a double-amputee frog.

Operation

I F someday soon we face a shortage of doctors, blame Milton Bradley's Operation, which taught a generation that one slip of the hand in a body cavity meant a super-annoying *buzzzz*. Oh, and also bloody death.

Operation laid open poor ol' Cavity Sam, and junior Dr. Frankensteins grabbed the tweezers and set to organ-thieving torture. Sam's injuries had apparently been sketched out by someone who'd never seen an anatomy textbook—"writer's cramp" was depicted by a tiny pencil, and "bread basket," by a piece of toast. The grandpa-era medical terms were cute, but they might as well have been Cockney. Water on the knee? Charley horse? Smartly, in 2003, Milton Bradley allowed fans to vote for a new weird ailment for Sam, and the winner was the brilliant "brain freeze," depicted by an ice-cream cone in the head.

The game actually came with rules, cards, and even fake money, but that was beyond the point. It was all about avoiding the *buzzzz*, as if it were a multimillion-dollar malpractice lawsuit. There was always one kid, however, who reveled in the eardrum-scratching sound and intentionally pressed the tweezers against the metal sides until he was clobbered over the head with a nearby Connect Four stand.

X-TINCTION RATING: Still going strong.

FUN FACT: The classic box shows a doctor dropping his cigarette ashes into the patient. The cig was snuffed from future box art.

Original Taco Doritos

Y ES, there are approximately eight thousand Doritos flavors, and four thousand of them have used the word "taco" in some way. There was Zesty Taco. There was Tacos at Midnight, which apparently self-destruct if they're eaten at any other time of day. But none of those strange chemical combinations exactly re-created the most-longed-for Doritos flavor of all time, 1967's original Taco flavor.

While Nacho Cheese became known as the chip's basic flavor, Taco actually came first. It was a spicy, fresh-tasting chip that was reminiscent of the spices used to season taco meat. It bravely ventured forth onto store shelves in an era when both tortilla chips and tacos were still as exotic as escargot and curry, and then suddenly, it vanished.

And then, in January 2011—an apparent miracle. Bags bearing the retro design of the long-missed Taco chip started showing up in grocery stores, and Frito-Lay announced that the original seasoning blend had returned, if only for a limited time. Fans love the old-fashioned bag, but those we pulled are split on whether the taste matches their memories.

X-TINCTION RATING: Revised and revived.
REPLACED BY: Frito-Lay has launched numerous taco-related chips, but true fans claim that the flavor has never been the same since the 1970s.

The Osmonds

MARIE was a little bit country, Donny was a little bit rock and roll, and the entire Osmond family was all teeth, family values, and flared pants. And for a kid in the '70s, they were also a tough act to follow. In their TV specials, their variety shows, and even their short-lived 1972 cartoon, the clean-cut Utah siblings would good-naturedly josh each other, a foreign concept to those of us brought up on a steady diet of noogies, wedgies, and whatever it's called when your brother takes his middle knuckle and grinds it into your chest.

That was never more apparent than in the Osmonds' holiday specials, when eleventy million members of the Osmond clan would gather to ride horses in the snow, trade corny jokes, and sing, all the while looking Stepfordly ecstatic to be together. Kids watching at home missed much of the Osmond family fun; most were otherwise engaged—pulling hair, punching throats, and grating each other's face into the carpet.

Our distraught moms didn't understand why we couldn't emulate the Osmonds, who never resorted to such violent shenanigans. From older siblings Alan, Wayne, Merrill, and Jay to younger heartthrobs Donny and Marie, and even down to runty Jimmy, they were a family to envy, with their Mormon values and blindingly white smiles. Sure, a good portion of them were interchangeable (Quick, which one was Merrill?), but that just reinforced the notion that the Osmond whole was greater than the sum of its pearly-white parts.

X-TINCTION RATING: Still going strong. Donny took home the gold on *Dancing with the Stars* in 2009, and Alan's eight sons are in the biz, touring as the Osmonds—Second Generation.

FUN FACT: Oldest brothers Virl and Tom, who were deaf, didn't perform with the group but showed up from time to time on the family's Christmas specials.

Pay Phones

R ING, *ring*. Who's there? A booth full of awesome. The phone booth was your own little glass-and-steel getaway where you could make a call in private—or just pretend to be Clark Kent. For three minutes, anyway, until the mean old operator demanded more change.

Most high schools had at least one, and on big-city streets, the booths were lined up like a boxy metal Stonehenge. The phone books were on chains, as if that deterred thieves. Whatever—whenever you needed a piece of information, someone had already ripped out that page. But you were going to do it, too, so somehow that made it OK.

We'd drop in the dime (and eventually, in the '80s, a quarter) and listen for the satisfying clink. We'd always—always—stick our finger into the coin-return door, just in case. And sometimes we'd even get lucky. Thanks for the free change, Ma Bell slot machine. We were so entranced with the convenience of it all, we didn't think about how many people had punched the buttons before us with their grubby fingers or, worse, slobbered on the handset. If you listened closely, you could almost hear the germs.

X-TINCTION RATING: Gone for good—mostly.

REPLACED BY: Most of us now have cell phones and use them to shout very loudly at people in restaurants and in line at the supermarket.

Pen Pals

HAVING a pen pal opened up the world. You found one from places like a comic-book mailbag, the pen-pal exchange on *Big Blue Marble*, or the Trixie Belden fan club, and sent off a letter. We picked our pen pals based on purely scientific criteria—a cool first name, a common love for Rick Springfield, or a residence in a fascinating place. (Kids in Hawaii must have been overwhelmed with mainlanders wanting to correspond.) An active writer could have two, three, or even a half dozen pen-pal relationships going at once. Waiting for the mailman suddenly became fun.

Our letters laid out our twelve-year-old hearts. We exchanged school pictures, wailed about classes, and confided about our crushes. We showed off our neato Care Bear stationery and covered the envelope with scratch 'n' sniff popcorn stickers, dotted our i's with giant hearts, and sketched elaborate swirls under our signature. We traded regional slang (Boston pen pals were "wicked cool") and shared mix tapes of local bands. We were never likely to meet this person so far away, so we could display a confidence in writing that we actually didn't have in our own school halls.

Eventually, of course, the letters slowed to a trickle and stopped. But before they did, we'd gotten to know someone outside our town, someone who got grounded or dumped and who fought with his or her siblings just like we did. And we learned that kids in Hawaii or Ireland or Iowa were really a lot like us.

X-TINCTION RATING: Gone for good.
REPLACED BY: The innocence of preteen postal correspondence all but vanished as email replaced snail mail.
FUN FACT: We kids didn't quite get Charlie Brown's endless struggles to send an unblotted letter to his pen pal. Why didn't he just use a ballpoint?

Pepsi Light

WHO didn't like Dorothy Hamill with her sassy wedge haircut? Who doesn't like soda with a sassy wedge of lemon? Logically, Pepsi Light, Pepsi's first lemon-spiked cola, should have been a hit. But the oh-so-'80s soda vanished faster than Molly Ringwald on the first season of *The Facts of Life*, despite a catchy theme song that claimed "The time is right! For Pepsi Light! Lemony! Pepsi Light! We put a little lemony taste in and took out half the calories!"

Apparently, though, the time just wasn't right. Pepsi Light was introduced in 1975, but its light burned out around 1986. Maybe we Americans wanted to keep squeezing lemon wedges into our cola ourselves. Maybe, in a decade when zero- and one-calorie diet sodas were becoming as common as legwarmers, only taking out half the

calories wasn't enough (Pepsi eventually reintroduced the drink with only one calorie). Or maybe it was because the drink itself tasted like you'd polished the ice cubes with Lemon Pledge. One of those, we're pretty sure.

Since then, Pepsi's returned to the research lab again and again, offering such memorable and short-lived soft drink siblings as Crystal Pepsi, Pepsi Holiday Spice, and Windex look-alike Pepsi Blue. We eagerly await the eventual introduction of Plaid Pepsi, Jalapeño-Cilantro Pepsi, and that Christmastime specialty, Pepsi Pine.

X-TINCTION RATING: Gone for good.

REPLACED BY: In 2000 and 2001, Pepsi introduced new lemon colas, Pepsi Twist and Diet Pepsi Twist, which were gone by 2006. Pepsi has also offered the simply named Diet Pepsi Lemon, but only for a limited time. As long as life keeps giving Pepsi lemons, the company is bound and determined to keep making lemon cola.

Planters Cheez Balls

LOOK, we knew it wasn't real cheese. The "z" gave that away. But something about these orange-powdered spheres made junk-food junkies out of even health nuts. Who knew that Planters, a nut company, could slip in and beat Chester Cheetah at his own powdery orange game?

Their packaging was genius—they came in a tall blue tin with a peel-off lid. (Like pudding lids, it would cut you if you were careless. Mr. Peanut wasn't messin' around.) The cheese-powder-to-crunch ratio was impeccable, and the texture was perfect for sucking between your teeth, although too many could lead to a painful case of Cap'n Crunch Mouth. But best of all was the shape. They were small and round, like mothballs, perfect to huck across the junior-high cafeteria or to toss up in the air and catch in your mouth.

The original Cheez Balls came back as Cheez Mania in 1999, but the mania was short-lived. Kids must now return to whipping tuna sandwiches at each other.

X-TINCTION RATING: Gone for good.
REPLACED BY: Cheetos has a cheese ball called Asteroids, but please. Other powdered-cheese products just don't compare.

Plastic Models

WE should have known it wouldn't end well. Stricken with model fever, we'd visit the hobby shop, mouth agape at the thousands of kits stacked to the ceiling and the World War II bombers dangling from fishing line. We'd agonize over which one to pick: A '57 Chevy or a tank? The Creature from the Black Lagoon or a glow-in-the-dark Frankenstein? The anticipation was always palpable.

We'd eventually make our choice, and when we got home, we'd

meticulously lay everything out, carefully twist the little pieces off of their plastic trees, take a deep breath, and—like a ten-year-old brain surgeon—begin.

But there was a big difference between the finished model we'd built in our head and the soon-to-be-deformed thing on the table in front of us. Doing it right required patience, hand-eye coordination, and at least a semblance of skill, which we quickly realized we completely lacked. The tube of glue inevitably spurted all over everything, fusing the tiny model pieces to our fingers.

Still, we'd grind our teeth and forge through, all the while comparing the elaborate box art to our own pathetic effort. But no matter how hard we'd try, we always ended up with a lopsided plane, crooked decals, and a little glue-drenched pilot who couldn't see because of the giant thumbprint on the windshield.

X-TINCTION RATING: Still going strong.
FUN FACT: Kids in the '70s could combine two of their favorite model subjects, monsters and cars, with kits that featured Dracula driving a dragster or the Mummy zipping around in a hot rod.

Playing Outside

ONCE upon a time, before video games, activity-packed schedules, and news of abductions terrorized parents into handcuffing their kids to the house, children used to play outside. Yes, outside (Google it), with real air, bugs, weather, and other flesh-and-blood kids.

One step out the door, and we were gone. We would explore abandoned buildings, organize pickup games of touch football in a vacant lot, and play on piles of dirt that could easily pass for the dunes of Tatooine. We were unsupervised and on our own, and our imaginations thrived because of it.

We could be pirates or princesses, cowboys or Indians. We'd build elaborate forts with rusty nails and splintered boards. We'd catch salamanders in window wells. We'd make mud pies. We'd hop on our BMX bikes and pedal for miles, until we suddenly realized that we had an hour ride back home ahead of us. We'd play Spud, Capture the Flag, or Trench in the cul-de-sac for hours, until it got so dark we couldn't see one another anymore. We'd get bruises and bumps, grass stains, and scraped-up knees. Maybe someday they'll make a video game out of the idea.

X-TINCTION RATING: Gone for good.
REPLACED BY: Playing outdoors now has its own movement behind it: Take a Child Outside Week. In our day, that would have been as unnecessary as Feed Your Child Some Food Week or Inhale Some Air Week.

Pop Rocks

T'S like the Mad Libs of urban legends. Pick a brand-name candy (Pop Rocks) and a popular beverage (Coke). Add in a semifamous person no one has seen in a while (how about Mikey, from the Life cereal commercials?) and invent a creative death (he exploded!).

The details vary—it was a suicide attempt, or one of the other kids from the commercial challenged him to down a case of the candy followed by a six-pack of Coke. Either way, the end is the same—a gloriously gory eruption of entrails.

The fictional story of Mikey's dreadful demise only added to the lore of Pop Rocks, the candy that made you feel like you were licking an electric fence. The magic reaction had something to do with pressurized carbon dioxide, but really, just as we don't want to know that Mexican jumping beans are actually moth larvae, the science of the sweet is secondary.

Pop Rocks were more than a candy—they were a challenge. Bullies would dare other kids to swallow them, foreshadowing how, a decade later, those same kids would dare fellow frat boys to do twenty-one shots of Jäger on their twenty-first birthday. Some kids squirmed at the ensuing snaps, crackles, and pops, but for most kids, the only thing better than candy was candy that fought back.

X-TINCTION RATING: Still going strong.

FUN FACT: They now have a chocolate-dipped version, plus a candy cane–flavored limited edition for Christmas. You can also find Pop Rocks made into bubble gum and mixed into cereals and ice cream.

The Pop Shoppe

S MART sugar junkies ignored all the hubbub about the Pepsi Challenge and teaching the world to sing and turned instead to the red-and-white, painted-on labels of Pop Shoppe pop for their super-sweet beverage fix.

The reusable, stubby glass bottles came in red plastic cases and were only available at stand-alone Pop Shoppe stores. Forget ordinary six-packs of soda tied together with duck-strangling plastic hoops. Who wanted a half dozen cans of the same flavor, anyway? Pop Shoppe patrons could mix and match from a flavor list of nearly thirty choices—old standbys like orange and grape, and far more exotic options like pineapple and bubble gum.

And while the flavors tickled the taste buds, the Pop Shoppe stores had giant, clanky conveyer belts that tickled the imagination. How in the name of Rube Goldberg did such an industrial factory produce even one drop of such delicately sweet, fruity nectar? Magic, duh.

X-TINCTION RATING: Revised and revived.
REPLACED BY: The concept fizzled in the United States in 1983, but a revitalized Pop Shoppe is now making a splash in Canada.

Power Records Book-and-Record Sets

IN pre-VCR days, kids couldn't just pop in a movie whenever the mood struck. Book-and-record sets were the next best thing. You'd throw the record on your turntable and flop on your bedroom's orange shag carpet with the accompanying book spread out in front of you. Invisible Record Guy would set you up with some easy instructions that were oddly reminiscent of the A/V dorks at school: "When you hear this signal—*boop*—turn the page. All right?" You have yourself a deal, Invisible Record Guy!

Disneyland, Columbia, and other brands all offered the book-and-record combos. Some featured stand-alone books; others had giant books glued right inside a fold-out album sleeve. But the brand to beat all brands was Power Records, a division of famed kids' label Peter Pan. Aimed at slightly older kids than the other labels, Power featured comic-book and TV characters. We played *G.I. Joe: The Secret of the Mummy's Tomb* and *Spider-Man: Invasion of the Dragon Men* until the needle on our Fisher-Price record player was nothing but a nub.

Power also dramatized such literary classics as *The Last of the Mohicans* and *Robinson Crusoe*. It's entirely possible that one or two desperate kids tried to turn in an English 101 book report based purely on the Power Records version. Teachers always knew, of course. When you hear this signal—*boop*—you flunk.

> **X-TINCTION RATING:** Gone for good. Peter Pan retired the Power label in 1977.
>
> **REPLACED BY:** VCRs and then DVD players eventually let kids immerse themselves in multimedia experiences without having to turn a single page.
>
> **FUN FACT:** You can relive the Power Records experience through the magic of YouTube.

Pudding Pops

IN the 1980s, über TV dad Bill Cosby also served as a pitchman for Jell-O Pudding Pops. The Cos claimed Mom would approve of the frozen treats because they contained "all the goodness of real pudding." Which might have made sense in Bizarro World, where kids who didn't choke down at least one bite of pudding were sent to bed without their broccoli, but never quite played in Actual World, in which pudding, frozen or otherwise, was just as much of a rare

privilege as staying up to watch Johnny Carson's monologue.

Whether it was the avalanche of Cosby-fueled advertising or their own delicious cracklike creaminess, Pudding Pops became the must-have freezer filler of the 1980s. Forget Fudgsicles and Otter Pops, not to mention that suggested serving size of "one," a bored and hungry kid could suck down a whole box of these things before the freezer door slammed shut.

Reportedly, Pudding Pops were dunked in water before being packaged, which left a gloriously thin coating of ice over each pop. Just like fish know from birth how to use their gills, kids knew instinctively how to dr-r-r-aaaag their incisors down the length of the pop, shattering the icy skin and shaving only a delicate layer of the chocolate, vanilla, or choco-vanilla swirl along with it. How's that for fine motor skills?

X-TINCTION RATING: Revised and revived.

REPLACED BY: Jell-O Pudding Pops were gobbled up in the 1990s, But the Jell-O name was later licensed to Popsicle, which reintroduced Jell-O Pudding Pops in 2004. Sadly, sharp-eyed eaters say it's just not the same. Popsicle uses a more rounded, pointy mold, and the beloved icy shell seems to have melted away in the interim. Freezer fanatics will note that the term "pudding pop" is not exclusive to one company—local brands also exist.

Quisp and Quake Cereals

F AMOUS pop-culture wars include Spy vs. Spy, Itchy vs. Scratchy, and, of course, Quisp vs. Quake. The sugary cereals tasted exactly the same, but creator Quaker Oats was smart enough to release them both in 1966 and set off a memorable advertising war that wouldn't end until Quake was voted out of existence in 1972.

Quisp, a tiny pink alien from the Planet Q, flew around via a beanie built into his head. He bragged that his flying saucer–shaped cereal was "vitamin powered." Which it probably was, if sugar is a vitamin. Strongman Quake's gear-shaped cereal was supposedly "earthquake powered." That doesn't really make sense, but apparently Ma and Pa Quaker were looking for any excuse to name all their kids something starting with the letter Q. No sense re-monogramming the towels.

Nothing was left but for the two tribes to go to war, which they did via a 1972 vote. The deck was stacked from the beginning: Who are kids going to love more, a dorky, cross-eyed li'l alien, or a muscly miner? Quisp won in a landslide, and the official Quaker line was

that Quake retreated back into his underground mines. (He resurfaced a few years later as an Australian cowboy hawking Quake's Orange Quangaroos.) Quisp had little time to savor his victory—his cereal sailed home to Planet Q by the end of the 1970s. But like John Travolta, this 1970s icon would eventually strut back into the limelight.

X-TINCTION RATING (QUAKE): Gone for good.

X-TINCTION RATING (QUISP): Revived and revised.

REPLACED BY: In 1999, noticing that now-grown-up kids still held fond memories of Quisp, Quaker reintroduced it via Quisp.com. You can still buy it there, and it's also in some supermarkets.

Rankin/Bass Stop-Action TV Specials

THEY weren't cartoons, and they sure weren't live-action or claymation. Rankin/Bass's stop-action TV specials were immediately recognizable and always just a little weird. The characters walked as if their ginormous bobbleheads might fall off their neck stalks at any moment, and even the evil dudes had doe-like, googly Muppet eyes that made it hard to take their villainy seriously.

The plots were positively Krofftian in their insanity, and keeping them straight was impossible. Was it *Rudolph* or *Santa Claus Is Comin' to Town* that featured Hermey, the elf who wanted to be a dentist? Was that the same one with the Island of Misfit Toys? Which one had Burgermeister Meisterburger? Heat Miser and Snow Miser? Eh, who cares? They were awesome.

Not all the specials were Christmas-themed. *Here Comes Peter Cottontail* celebrated Easter. And *Mad Monster Party* was that rare bird indeed—a Halloween special, remembered best for chesty, redheaded bombshell Francesca. But all Rankin/Bass specials shared a cheerful, aw-shucks outlook and a fierce love for the underdog that resonated with kids. We're all misfit toys at heart.

X-TINCTION RATING: Gone for good. But many of the classic specials are still running on TV during the holidays.

REPLACED BY: Stop-action has gotten slick and fancy—see *Coraline* and *Fantastic Mr. Fox*—but the goofy charm of the Rankin/Bass days is still missed.

Real People and That's Incredible!

B ACK when reality shows were still fresh and new, watching them didn't make you want to scrub yourself raw with a Brillo pad. NBC's *Real People* kicked off the trend in 1979 by combining taped features with interviews in front of a live studio audience.

Preternaturally perky Sarah Purcell and Skip Stephenson played the flirty mom and dad to an ever-expanding gaggle of correspondents (including a young Peter Billingsley, who would go on to shoot his eye out as Ralphie in *A Christmas Story*), who reported from such breaking-news hotspots as turkey-calling contests, zucchini festivals, and roller coasters. If not for *Real People*, how would Americans have known about the eighty-five-year-old Oklahoma waitress who hosted a popular radio show from a phone booth?

In 1980, ABC leaped into the reality fray, introducing *That's Incredible!*, which featured more stunts than human-interest stories. Yep, it had knife jugglers and a guy catching a bullet in his mouth. But the random collection of big-haired hosts was its greatest appeal: John Davidson, Cathy Lee Crosby, and Minnesota Viking great Fran Tarkenton in the same room at the same time? And people wanted to watch? That really *was* incredible.

X-TINCTION RATING: Gone for good.
REPLACED BY: Reality shows abound, but they've wandered far afield from the sweet ditziness of Sarah Purcell interviewing a guy who did backflips for a quarter.

Record Players

A S a kid, you had two choices if you wanted to listen to your beloved copy of Meco's disco-riffic *Star Wars and Other Galactic Funk* LP over and over again. You could plead with your older brother to let you use the record player in his room. Or you could take the route that didn't end in a punch in the arm: ask Santa for the holy grail of middle-school music players—the almighty Fisher-Price record player.

Record players were amazing things. No wonder your older brother protected his precious stereo equipment like it was a bag full of weed. The record would drop, and the arm would fluidly leap into action—a little robot that loved Supertramp.

When your brother wasn't around, you'd kick up the speed to 78 RPM and make Rush sound like a hard-driving Alvin and the Chipmunks. You'd also take the liberty to play a 45, but since you were too lazy to go find the little plastic snap-in adapter, the record would stagger as it spun, as if it had just downed a six-pack of record beer.

The kid-friendlier Fisher-Price player was portable, which meant you could cart it to parties or sleepovers. Eventually, Fisher-Price introduced an even-more-portable battery-powered version, which let kids pretend they were Wolfman Jack anytime or anyplace—on a camping trip, in the car, during a power outage—as long as the Duracells held out.

X-TINCTION RATING: Gone for good.

REPLACED BY: Audiophiles and club DJs keep the turntable dream alive, but most folks left vinyl behind years ago. And most kids today have their own MP3 players, plus no real idea where the expression "like a broken record" came from.

Rock 'Em Sock 'Em Robots

BACK when parents weren't the least bit concerned about buying murderous toys for their kids, three-dimensional boxing game Rock 'Em Sock 'Em Robots was all about the vicarious violence. We couldn't haul off on our brother in the living room (not without a spanking, anyway), but we could face off in the ring. Two kids would grip joysticks positioned on either side of the toy, and their plastic proxies would beat the nuts and bolts out of each other, uppercutting and jabbing with such verve that the boxing ring would often lift right off the table. Ah, the satisfying *kzzzz* as your robotic rival's head popped into the air. Even more satisfying: hearing your opponent wail, "You knocked my block off!"

Kids loved the instant gratification: You pressed the plunger, the robot moved. You bobbed and weaved, so did your 'bot. Rock 'Em Sock 'Em was the red-and-teal plastic ancestor of the modern video game, preparing us for a future full of brightly colored killing machines that, thankfully, never came to be. It did teach important lessons, though, like how to settle conflict, that getting smacked in the jaw had consequences, and, most important, that robotic decapitation was a whole lot of fun.

X-TINCTION RATING: Revised and revived.

REPLACED BY: Mattel came out with a new—although oddly smaller—version of the classic toy in 2001, inspiring a new generation to knock each other's block off.

Roller Rinks

THE lights were dim, the music was thumpin', and the pants were tight. Your local roller rink was a cross between a bowling alley and a Persian prince's palace: Every surface was covered in carpet, and it smelled a little bit like cloves.

Birthday parties and weekends were happily spent getting dizzy at joints like the Skatin' Place, Skate Teen, and Skate World. The biggest challenge: finding just the right second to step into the swirling current of skaters. Time it perfectly, or like a newbie hockey player, you'd get checked into the boards.

Once we were rolling wobbly along, we'd act out scenes from *Xanadu* and marvel at the high-tech mood-setting wizardry, which included strobe lights, disco balls, and dry ice. Gaggles of teenage girls dressed in rainbow shirts would shuffle by in clumps, holding hands and giggling. Hotshot figure skaters with feathered Farrah hair would scream past, then twirl in circles in the free-skate area of the rink. Depending on the year, we did the Hustle, grooved to "A Fifth of Beethoven," or sang along with "Mickey" at the top of our adolescent lungs. When the terrifying Couples Skate came up, we suddenly found it the perfect time to hide out in the bathroom.

We'd limp home six hours later, feet raw, hopped up on Sugar Babies, and giddy with momentum—and ready to roll back and do it all again.

X-TINCTION RATING: Gone for good.
REPLACED BY: A few roller rinks still cling to life, but most enthusiasts now do their skating outside, using in-line skates.

FUN FACT: *CHiPs* set a pair of completely awesome episodes at a roller disco in 1979.

Rondo Soda

RONDO soda, available from 1978 into the 1980s, was kind of like the weird new kid in school who actually turns out to be pretty cool. It was a citrus soda, and citrus was always the class geek next to the cheerleaders of the cola world. It also dressed kinda funny, in a yellow can decked out with a lemon tree and old-fashioned writing. Rondo looked less like pop and more like a lemon-based patent medicine created in the *Magnificent Ambersons* era.

But Rondo almost made up for its geekiness with its fresh, sweet taste and its commercials. The ads showed two guys doing something manly and working up a "Rondo thirst." They then pounded down cans of Rondo, as if it were going to turn into battery acid if they didn't chug it in three seconds flat. The voice-over praised the drink not for its taste but for the fact that it was only lightly carbonated, "so you can slam it down fast." Yes, poor Rondo, whose main feature was apparently the speed with which it could be consumed.

X-TINCTION STATUS: Gone for good.
REPLACED BY: If you travel Down Under, try Australia's Solo, a lemon soda made by Rondo's parent company, Schweppes, which is reportedly very similar.

Roosevelt Franklin

SOME Muppets are permanent residents of *Sesame Street*—Oscar's past forty now, and you're never getting him outta that trash can. Roosevelt Franklin only lived on the Street for a few early seasons, but the engaging little guy forever hops on in fans' memories.

Roosevelt was a cool little guy with a striped shirt and black hair that stood up straight as a paintbrush. Was he a kid? He looked like one, and his mom appeared in some skits. Was he a teacher? He stood in front of the classroom and taught about Africa, or loud versus soft, or why you shouldn't call your friend Cantaloupe Head. Whatever his role, he was so beloved that the school where he taught/attended/hung out was named Roosevelt Franklin Elementary. Named for him or an ancestor? Homage or coincidence? Don't ask; it's a chicken-egg thing.

Muppets don't really have race—Roosevelt was purple—but he definitely spoke with African-American style. According to the fabulous *Sesame* history *Street Gang*, outside forces decided he promoted negative racial stereotypes and the character was quietly dumped. It's OK, Roosevelt. You were too cool for school anyway.

X-TINCTION RATING: Gone for good.

REPLACED BY: Though it's not really a true replacement, the cool school on *Sesame* these days is Abby Cadabby's Flying Fairy School, a recurring sketch that debuted in 2009.

FUN FACT: In 2008, Stephen Colbert held a mock debate on *The Colbert Report* to determine whether Theodore Roosevelt or Franklin Delano Roosevelt was the better Roosevelt. In the end, he awarded the title to Roosevelt Franklin.

Sassy Magazine

TIGER *Beat* hyped celebrities, and *Seventeen* was heavy on makeup and clothes. If those three things weren't the mainstays of your teen existence, the magazine rack was a pretty frustrating place—until 1988, when *Sassy* magazine blasted onto the scene.

Here was a teen magazine that didn't speak only to the cheerleaders and homecoming queens but reached out to the burnouts, the brains, and every girl who didn't believe that a new mascara would change her life. *Sassy* not only celebrated indie music but convinced girls that they just needed a garage and a guitar to start their own band. It reviewed zines and got alternative rockers to offer dating advice. Certain stars (Michael Stipe, onetime *Sassy* intern Chloë Sevigny) were favorites, but there was no kowtowing to the vapid celeb of the moment. (One article was headlined "23 Celebrities Not to Dress Like." Helllooooo, *Seventeen* fave Whitney Houston.)

Reading *Sassy* felt like talking to an über-cool big sister, and the writers encouraged that feeling by signing their articles with just their first names. Jane, Christina, Mary Kaye, and Margie didn't seem like ivory-tower editors in a Manhattan skyscraper but like trusted pals. When *Sassy* was sold (humiliatingly, to the company that published *Teen*) and eventually shut down, it wasn't like a magazine ended; it was like letters from your coolest friend simply stopped arriving.

X-TINCTION RATING: Gone for good.

REPLACED BY: No modern magazine is as cool, but *Sassy*'s alums, and those it influenced, are everywhere—running blogs, rocking out in bands, writing books. It was honored with a 2007 book, *How Sassy Changed My Life: A Love Letter to the Greatest Teen Magazine of All Time*.

FUN FACT: In a recurring *Saturday Night Live* sketch, Phil Hartman played a *Sassy* editor who hosted a talk show and used the word "sassy" in as many ways as he could.

Saturday Night Fever– Inspired Clothes

DEAR disco era: Thanks for the music. The clothes, though? What were you on?

Most Gen-X kids were too young to see 1977's *Saturday Night Fever* in theaters, but they were well aware of the iconic image of John Travolta striking a pose in his three-piece, skin-hugging white suit, finger pointed defiantly into the air and hip cocked like he'd thrown out his back. The famed picture was emblazoned on everything from T-shirts to trading cards, pins to giant belt buckles.

Knockoffs of Travolta's outfit were everywhere, including hang-

ing in our older siblings' closets, smelling vaguely like sweat, cigarettes, and Drakkar. Tony Manero wannabes teetered outside disco clubs on platform shoes, sporting painted-on dark shirts with collars sharp enough to draw blood and open enough to reveal a nest of chest hair cradling gold chains. The suits were so tight some '70s club-goers are now likely using the pants as support hose to prevent deep vein thrombosis. Sure, Travolta was nominated for an Oscar for his performance, but the real star of the movie was the white polyester suit.

X-TINCTION RATING: Gone for good.
REPLACED BY: All-white duds made a comeback in the mid-'80s thanks to Crockett and Tubbs from *Miami Vice*.

Schoolhouse Rock!

THE concept sounds horrible: Hey, kids! We're going to pepper your Saturday TV time with learning! But if a whole generation knows the Preamble to the Constitution or the order of the planets or that fat cigar-smoking cats shouldn't be allowed in pool halls, they can thank the happy little family of videos called *Schoolhouse Rock!*

As with the *Brady Bunch* siblings, certain members of the family were overhyped. "Conjunction Junction" and "I'm Just a Bill" overshadowed the Jan-like charms of kangaroo-adopting, pronoun-hawking "Rufus Xavier Sarsaparilla" or the dreamy ice skater in "Figure Eight." And *Schoolhouse Rock!* created as many questions as it answered. What kind of camp sent kids unpacking their adjectives near a hairy, scary bear? Was that youngest Lolly really old enough to be slaving away in an adverb store? Who got beat up worse, the football player in "Interjections" who threw the wrong way, or the Poindexter who cheered, "Hurray! I'm for the other team"?

Still, the tunes sank into kids' brains like grape jelly into Wonder bread, and we would be a better nation today if older folks, too, had their own versions. Imagine *Schoolhouse Rock!* songs for such topics as "Floss! That's What's Happening" and "Lolly, Lolly, Lolly, Get Your Adjustable Rate Subprime Mortgages Here." Well, maybe not that one.

X-TINCTION RATING: Revised and revived.

REPLACED BY: The original creators helped put out a 2009 environmentally themed collection, *Schoolhouse Rock! Earth*.

FUN FACT: The late jazz singer Blossom Dearie's voice can be heard in "Unpack Your Adjectives," "Mother Necessity," and the haunting "Figure Eight."

Scratch 'n' Sniff Stickers

WHAT does a rainbow smell like? How about a cowboy boot? Rope? Bone? A computer? Pilgrims? Stars? *Space?* Kids might not know, but with one scrape of a fingernail across a scratch 'n' sniff sticker, they could sure find out. (The answers? Plastic, leather, plastic, plastic, plastic, plastic, soap, and plastic.)

Scratch 'n' sniff stickers exploded like a sneeze in the 1970s and 1980s. Teachers stuck them on assignments that made the grade, kids plastered them on their Trapper Keepers, and harried parents scraped them off bedroom doors. Sweet scents dominated, but daring kids were drawn to the savory stickers, even though "pizza" smelled less like tomatoes and pepperoni and more like a late-night burp.

Best were the completely random or gross-out scents, often of items you'd never think to smell: the coconut ghost, the custard-scented egg, the stickers labeled "old shoe" or "onion." Also, sticker makers seemed to envision a kid populace that loved black licorice much more than was actually the case. But no one can knock their smell longevity: Decades after the fad cooled, old stickers still cling to their scents like Tootie to her roller skates.

X-TINCTION RATING: Still going strong.

FUN FACT: Stinky stickers still abound, with SmellStickers.com doing its best to bring back the 1980s craze in true retro style.

Sea-Monkeys

JUMPIN' Jiminy Cricket, they looked like us. Or at least what we'd look like after a few generations spent mating with Pokémon characters. We first fell in love with Sea-Monkeys via their classic ads in comic books, which featured tantalizingly colorful images of a family of pink creatures—all long, gangly limbs, smiling faces, and twisty tails. "Own a bowlful of happiness!" the headlines screamed.

More like a bowlful of disappointment. When the critters showed up in the mail, eager kids ripped open the packets, mixed the contents with water, and waited patiently for a new society to emerge from the murk.

Alas, no amount of wishing was going to turn the Sea-Monkeys into anything other than what they actually were: barely noticeable brine shrimp that, when mixed with water, wriggled around like teeny tiny bugs. The cruddy crustaceans would eventually end up getting tipped over and falling to their deaths after their owners grew weary of the reality of their pointless existence. How many carpets from the '70s have dried-up Sea-Monkeys entombed among their fibers? Probably all of them.

X-TINCTION RATING: Still going strong.

FUN FACT: While the Sea-Monkeys themselves have a life span of about two years, the brand has been around for five decades.

Seven Up Bar

PERFECT for the indecisive kid, Pearson's Seven Up bar took all the option paralysis out of choosing a candy. Unrelated to the Uncola, the bar must have been created by a real people-pleaser who just couldn't stand to leave one flavor unrepresented. Butterscotch! Cherry! Fudge! Coconut! Orange! Nougat! Buttercream! Aaugh, I can't decide, just cram them *all* in there! The flavors even changed over the years—older snackers fondly remember Brazil nut and maple walnut centers.

The bar was kind of like a chocolate-covered row house, with tiny walls of chocolate separating each tasty dwelling. It was not the choice of picky eaters or those who didn't care for coconut or turned up their noses at cherry. But for those who never felt the need to poke their fingers into each Valentine's Day chocolate and throw away half of them uneaten, here was your candy. Sweet.

X-TINCTION RATING: Gone for good.

REPLACED BY: Pearson's stopped making Seven Up in the 1970s. But if you really need a flavor fix, Necco makes the Sky Bar, which has four sections—caramel, peanut, vanilla, and fudge. Hey, we're halfway there.

Shakey's Pizza

I N those prehistoric days before you could make a call and have some dude deliver a steaming pizza straight to your door, the best way to get a fix of molten cheese and yeasty dough was to head to the neighborhood pizza parlor. And no destination was higher on a kid's wish list than Shakey's Pizza.

Long tables and wooden signs with a ye olde font set the mood. And ubiquitous player pianos and banjo pluckers burned a love—or horrible distaste—for ragtime music into a generation's collective consciousness. Shakey's thrived during a simpler time. Something as basic as a window into the kitchen kept kids' attention for hours on end.

Could you get your average high-school kid to work at a place like this today? With all the striped shirts, straw hats, and ice-pick-to-the-head music, it might be tough to find employees outside of a Future Barbershop Quarteters of America convention.

X-TINCTION RATING: Still going strong, although today only about sixty locations exist in the United States, down from five hundred.

The Shazam!/Isis Hour

THE show was about an old guy wearing a turtleneck and driving around in a tricked-out RV with a teenage boy he wasn't related to. What's wrong with that? Before *Superman: The Movie* convinced us a man could fly, the considerably lower-budget Saturday-morning *Shazam!/Isis Hour* made us fairly aware that a guy could kind of look like he was sort of up in the air. A little.

Still, what cooler fantasy for a kid than to instantly turn grownup and super-powered by uttering a single word? When Billy Batson yelled "Shazam!" an animated bolt from the heavens transformed the teen into Captain Marvel, much cooler than Clark Kent dropping trou in a phone booth.

The setup was simple: Billy and his mentor (Name: Mentor) traveled the country (OK, just the San Fernando Valley), righting wrongs and sometimes teaming up with fellow hero Isis, a hot teacher who invoked her magic amulet and turned into a gorgeous Egyptian goddess. After uttering "Oh mighty Isis!" she took off her glasses and let her hair down, looking suspiciously like another Wonderful Woman.

Both heroes took a nonviolent tack and spent their respective half hours helping goofballs who got themselves into dangerous situations, then wrapped it all up with a tidy little moral. Fine, but we'd rather somebody got punched.

X-TINCTION RATING: Gone for good.
REPLACED BY: *Shazam* carries on as a comic; *Isis* is out on DVD.

Short-Lived Sugary Cereals

WHY didn't our moms just sit us down at the breakfast table with the sugar bowl, a four-pack of food coloring, and a spoon? We probably would have ended up with the same ingredients in our bellies as we did consuming the sugary cereals of our youth.

We're not saying the 1970s and 1980s invented bad-for-you cereals, but that was when the breakfast industry went completely off the rails. Every character, movie, and game suddenly busted out with one. Rainbow Brite cereal had little edible rainbows. Mr. T cereal offered bowlfuls of a single letter—guess which one. Donkey Kong cereal featured barrels. Pac-Man cereal had marshmallow ghosts, marshmallow Pac-Man, *and* marshmallow Ms. Pac-Man with the little bow in her hair. For some reason, C-3POs were shaped like beer-can pull tabs, but the *Star Wars* in-box premiums more than made up for it.

Sometimes the cereal's expiration date outlived the fad it was named for. A prime example: Urkel-Os, strawberry-banana-flavored cereal named for the *Family Matters* geek with hiked-up pants and an even higher voice. We're betting people forgot who Urkel was before they even finished the box.

X-TINCTION RATING: Revised and revived.

REPLACED BY: These days, the cereal industry seems to lean more toward changing up old standards (Cupcake Pebbles, Halloween Crunch), but fads can still create a cereal. Witness 2009's High School Musical cereal, with star-shaped pieces.

FUN FACT: International fast-food chain Cerealicious serves up a wide variety of cereal choices plus smoothies and other items, all incorporating cereal.

Shrinky Dinks

INVENTED in 1973, Shrinky Dinks brought into play the one appliance that Mom never really wanted you to mess with: the oven. In fact, the whole Shrinky Dink process seemed kind of like a joyous, don't-tell-the-parents experiment. Melting plastic on a hot cookie sheet without getting yelled at? Sign us up!

Shrinky Dinks never looked like they were going to work. You colored in the shape, be it a Smurf, Mr. T, or a rainbow-maned unicorn, threw it on a cookie sheet, and hoped for the best. Watching through the oven door, you were convinced you'd done it wrong and nothing would ever happen when suddenly it started to curl up like an old sheet of fax paper. It twisted, and then it fixed itself, and the end product was tiny, bright and colorful, and thick and strong. As with Homer Simpson and his Flaming Moe drink, fire made it good.

Few kids really knew what to do with Shrinky Dinks once they were shrunky dunk. One can only have so many zipper pulls, key chains, and napkin rings, after all. But no one ever thought about that when they were watching the plastic writhe in its little kitchen torture chamber. Sometimes the journey is indeed way more fun than the destination.

X-TINCTION RATING: Still going strong.
FUN FACT: In the 1970s, superheroes were the bestselling Shrinky Dinks theme; in the 1980s, it was the Smurfs.

Sideshows

BY the time kids of the '70s and '80s were old enough to go to fairs and carnivals, the sideshows of earlier days were already a dying breed. The world had started to become sensitive to the idea that people shouldn't be exhibited under signs branding them "Mule-Faced Woman" or "The Living Torso," and the attractions were grudgingly changing. More fire-eaters, fewer freaks.

But for kids, sneaking down the midway to the sideshow tents still felt like a forbidden thrill, and some traveling shows delivered. Fat ladies, midgets, and bearded ladies—these were still considered OK to exploit, as was the occasional Lobster Boy, with flipper-like hands and feet. The Headless Centerfold illusion arranged a sexy bikini-clad girl so that her head was hidden and weird medical tubing took its place. The Girl-to-Gorilla act crammed spectators into a dark tent where they watched a curvy silhouette behind a curtain slowly transform into a huge ape shape. You didn't have too much time to judge this one closely because the guy in the ape suit would pretend to break out, and everyone would run shrieking from the tent.

Yes, the show was pretty much over by the time we were allowed to buy a ticket, but kids let their freak flag fly in other ways, mostly by sneaking books out of the library to gawk at photos of the Elephant Man and various Siamese twins.

X-TINCTION RATING: Revised and revived.
REPLACED BY: While the traditional freak show is gone for good, some traveling shows now promote a more illusion-based concept. And the Jim Rose Circus has featured a variety of circus stunts, such as sword swallowing, along with heavily tattooed and pierced personnel.

Silver Spoons

FOR a while there, it seemed like every kid on TV hit the parent lottery and ended up being raised by mega-rich adults: Arnold and Willis moved in with Mr. Drummond, Webster bunked with the Papadapolises, and Ricky Stratton left military school to room with his multimillionaire dad.

The premise of *Silver Spoons*, which ran from 1982 to 1987, was tailor-made for kids who dreamed about trading in their regular lives for an unlimited Toys "R" Us expense account and a chance to play with diamond-encrusted Ataris and use hundred-dollar bills for scratch paper. Blond moppet Ricky Stratton acted like comicdom's Richie Rich, and heck, actor Ricky Schroder even looked like him. His castle-like mansion was packed to the very expensive rafters with arcade games, a rideable train, and even—in one episode—Mr. T.

Ricky had hangers-on—a preteen *Entourage*, of sorts. Alfonso Ribeiro breakdanced a lot, and Jason Bateman's Derek was Eddie Haskell to Ricky's Beav. (Derek was so jerky, Ricky once told him he understood why all of his gerbils committed suicide.) Like most shows in the '80s, *Spoons* featured plenty of Very Special Episodes, covering everything from child abuse to drinking to kidnapping. All perfect stage-setting for Schroder's eventual stint as a cop on *NYPD Blue*.

X-TINCTION RATING: Gone for good but available on DVD. Schroder and Bateman are still working actors. In fact, so is Mr. T.
FUN FACT: Schroder changed his name to Rick in a bid to be taken more seriously but changed it back to Ricky in 2007.

Simon

FOR a short period of time in America, a stubby, bossy dictator named Simon held the nation in his sway, always harshly cutting them off and telling them they were wrong. *American Idol* judge Simon Cowell? Well, yes. But back in 1978, there was Simon, the mouthy electronic game.

Simon looked so simple. You just had to repeat a sequence in your head and slam your palm down on the right colors. Blue, blue, green! Blue, blue, green, yellow! Blue, blue, green, yellow, gr—*buzzz*! *"Auuugh! Red, I meant red!"*

Simon was uncheatable and unforgiving. You got better, he got faster. You mastered one sequence, he spat out a longer one. You shoved him under the couch and sulked, he laughed silently and waited you out.

Simon was a gateway drug. Kids never knew that they had voluntarily donned the yoke of future servitude to the machines. Soon, those same brains would race to learn the latest Pac-Man screen or memorize the sequence required to rip out their opponent's spinal cord in Mortal Kombat. In retrospect, Simon's genial tones ring with the simplicity of church bells.

X-TINCTION RATING: Still going strong.

FUN FACT: New versions of Simon include key-chain and pocket-sized editions, so you can now carry your frustration around with you.

Sitting in the Way Back of a Station Wagon

BACK in the days before safety was invented, the most sought-after seat in Mom's faux-wood-paneled Country Squire station wagon wasn't shotgun in the front. It wasn't in the back, either, crammed in with your sticky siblings. It was the "way back"—vehicular Valhalla. While the rest of the family faced front, the luckiest kids scored the best seats in the house, the collapsible ones with a view out the rear window. Seat belts? Who needed 'em? When Dad took a hairpin turn, you'd roll around like a pop can.

But dang, what a ride. It was our own little space, like a tiny office or a Pullman bunk on a train. And the best part was that it put you as far away from your parents as the engineers in Detroit could possibly figure out. You were on your own little vacation, and if you wanted to stick your tongue out or make faces at cars behind you, who would know? Even though you were eight years old, you were still ahead of the poor slob driving behind you—who no doubt had his own kid facing out the back, making faces at yet another frustrated driver.

X-TINCTION RATING: Gone for good.
REPLACED BY: With the introduction of minivans, station wagons' popularity crashed.

Six Million Dollar Man Action Figure

STEVE Austin was a lucky man. And not because those military doctors saved his life when his experimental aircraft tumbled into a fiery ball of grainy stock footage. No, he was fortunate enough to have his accident back in the 1970s: Had he been injured today, his six-million-dollar repair budget would have gotten him a Band-Aid for his torn-off arm and a get-well card.

Yes, Colonel Austin fared pretty well, what with all the bionic whatnots and whoozits six million Carter-era bucks bought. His action figure was even cooler, with a huge eye for kids to look

through, a button on the back that ratcheted up his arm, and his best feature: the peel-back rubber skin on his forearm that revealed removable circuits beneath. Kids across the country spent hours making the *doot-doot-doot* bionic sound effect and forcing the Austin doll to put his sporty red jumpsuit and tennis shoes to good use and jog in slow motion around the ottoman.

His entourage? Less impressive. The Oscar Goldman figure, a fairly accurate rendition of Steve's balding boss at the OSI, came with a polyester sport coat, a briefcase that exploded if you opened it wrong, and a manila folder. What kid wouldn't want a thirteen-inch government bureaucrat as part of his toy collection? Snore as Goldman talks on the phone! Sigh as he pressures an underling into working late! Shrug as he cuts line items from his budget! Truly, the world's first inaction figure.

X-TINCTION RATING: Gone for good.
REPLACED BY: Transformers and GoBots eventually filled kids' need for robotic action figures.

Slime

MATTEL couldn't have hit on a product that was a better fit for its key demographic if there had been a gaggle of nine-year-old boys running its R&D department. Boogers in a garbage can? Slime was the mucusy holy grail of rude, crude playthings.

Slime was slooshy, splorfy greenish goo that would make incredibly satisfying fart sounds if you popped it the right way. The cold, clammy gloop could be squished between your fingers or dangled over your little brother's face, stretching ever closer and closer to his pursed lips like some alien maple syrup–mucus hybrid. The smell—mossy, fecund, and oddly chemical—lingers in a generation's sense memory. Even if it was safely back in its plastic slime can, the odor Slime left behind on hands was not unlike what remained after you'd been petting a wet dog all afternoon.

X-TINCTION RATING: Revised and revived.

REPLACED BY: Slime keeps squirming its way back onto toy store shelves. Mattel reintroduced the stuff in 2002—including a line with glittery colors and girlie carrying pouches designed to appeal to the fairer sex.

Snoopy Sno-Cone Machine

WHAT'S better, a toy or a snack? A toy that makes snacks. Introduced in 1979, the Snoopy Sno-Cone Machine wasn't the first food-preparation toy—the Easy-Bake oven dates to 1963—but it was, literally and figuratively, the coolest.

First, you mixed the sugar shock–inducing flavor syrup in a Snoopy-shaped squeeze bottle and shoved a regular ice cube into a hole in a big plastic doghouse. Then the fun part was pretty much over, and the sweatin' began. The TV commercials made shaving the ice cube look as easy as sharpening a pencil, but after about ten turns of the unwieldy plastic crank, most kids just gave up and whined until Mom agreed to do it.

Once the ice was finally transmogrified, things just kept on getting bleaker. The sno-cones looked large and luscious on the box, but in reality, they filled up teeny white paper cups so small they could serve Jell-O shots to Raggedy Ann. Kids in northern climes were known to just wait until winter, collect a big ol' bowl full of snow from outside, and squirt the Super Snoopy syrup on that instead. But none of the cruel reality interfered with the irrational lust kids held for this toy. Coveted by many, owned by few, it was a Sears Wish Book legend.

X-TINCTION RATING: Still going strong.
FUN FACT: Snoopy too sane for you? There's now a SpongeBob SquarePants Sno-Cone Maker. Good grief!

Spire Christian Comics, Featuring Archie

HEY, Mom brought home an Archie comic! Cool! Except this one gets a little weird, even for a guy whose best friend wears a crown and swallows hamburgers without chewing. Unlike the other comics in your collection, this has a distinctly churchy bent.

Halfway through a gag about computer dating, Betty (it's always Betty . . .) pulls out a Bible and goes on to bash modern movies, TV, and books. Or in a Wild West–themed story, schoolmarm Betty (again) tells Archie with horror that books now teach evolution. In other stories, Archie and the gang visit different planets, travel back in time to World War I, and become dragon-fighting knights, all in search of Jesus.

Turns out, Mom bought you a Spire Christian Comic. While it's a masterpiece of subtlety compared to the far more fundamentalist Jack T. Chick tracts—those little comiclike pamphlets that rail against things like rock music and evolution—it's not exactly the Laff-a-Lympics of Reggie pranks and Veronica-Lodge-is-*so*-rich jokes you were expecting. Written and drawn by Archie artist Al Hartley, a born-again Christian, this series may have had its heart in the right place, but reading it unawares was like falling asleep during Saturday morning cartoons and waking up to find that Tom and Jerry were now running *The 700 Club*.

X-TINCTION RATING: Gone for good.

REPLACED BY: Although there are certainly other Christian comics and graphic novels, Spire no longer publishes, and Archie mostly stays out of church.

Star Search

S OME think of it as *American Idol* without Paula Abdul but with the Publishers Clearing House guy. But oh, *Star Search* was so much more than that. From 1983 to 1995, a tuxedoed Ed McMahon herded singers, dancers, comedians, and spokesmodels on stage like performing monkeys with shoulder pads, teased hair, and plastered-on smiles.

After they sang, danced, joked, or looked pretty, the two competitors in each category had to stand right next to each other on stage as they heard how many stars the judges awarded them. The loser's fake so-happy-for-you grimace proved that it wasn't just the spokesmodels who could use lessons in acting.

What was a spokesmodel, anyway? The weird little videos showing them in various outfits and awkward poses seemed like auditions for a gig in a JCPenney catalog. When Ed handed his mic over to the candidates, they inevitably stumbled over such challenging cue-card statements as "We'll be right back after this."

Unlike *Idol*, *Star Search* spared the contestants the indignity of having to listen to the judges berate specific aspects of their performance in front of millions of people. On Ed's watch, no one was ever called "pitchy." Four out of four stars.

X-TINCTION RATING: Revised and revived.

REPLACED BY: *Star Search* came back in 2003 on CBS, hosted by Arsenio Hall.

FUN FACT: *Star Search* lived up to its name, finding an awful lot of aspiring singers and comedians who later became enormously famous. Britney Spears, Jessica Simpson, Justin Timberlake, Christina Aguilera, Adam Sandler, Rosie O'Donnell, Ray Romano, and Ellen DeGeneres all competed for America's love. Sadly, very few spokesmodels went on to find similar fame.

The Star Wars Holiday Special

THE prospect of 1978's *Star Wars Holiday Special* was enough to make our light sabers tingle with glee—a bonus chapter of the tale as we eagerly waited for the Empire to strike back. In practice, though, it was a disaster of intergalactic proportions. The plot, such as it was, focused on Chewbacca's family—his wife Malla, son Lumpy, and freakish (and, no doubt, flea-ridden and stinky) father Itchy—as they waited for Chewie to return home.

The original *Star Wars* gang made perfunctory appearances, including an overly made-up Mark Hamill and a stumbly Carrie Fisher. And it all spiraled even further into surreal territory when Bea Arthur, Art Carney, and Harvey Korman showed up. The special was so embarrassing that it only aired once. Thank the Force someone was forward-thinking enough to record it so that future generations could revel in this pile of Wookiee poo.

At least it didn't start a trend of other ill-advised holiday specials based on '70s movies. Who would have tuned in to *The Jaws Memorial Day Picnic Special* or *Rocky's Arbor Day Punching Extravaganza*? Oh, right: We would have.

X-TINCTION RATING: Still going strong.
FUN FACT: The TV special found a second life passed around from nerd to nerd on videotape, and now it's being terrible on an ongoing basis on the Internet.

Story Songs

THE unluckiest, and sometimes dumbest, people in the world lived in story songs. Wildfire's owner couldn't build a stall strong enough even for a pony. Billy, the would-be hero, wouldn't keep his head low despite it being the *only* thing his fiancée asked for. And don't even get us started on the girl in "Teen Angel," who apparently weighed "lose his class ring" against "possibly get squashed by a train" and chose the latter.

Unanswered questions abounded. What exactly was Billie Joe throwing off the Tallahatchie Bridge, besides himself? Would the crew of the *Edmund Fitzgerald* really have made Whitefish Bay if they'd put fifteen more miles behind her? What was the guy in "Tie a Yellow Ribbon" in jail for anyway? Did those guys in the mine really eat "Timothy"?

Sure, not all story songs were about death. "The Piña Colada Song" was about cheating on your woman, *with* your woman (whoops). "Half-Breed" was about how racism made Cher sleep around. "Gypsies, Tramps and Thieves" was about how poverty made

Cher sleep around. "Harper Valley PTA" was about how even hypocrites slept around. But damn if story songs didn't deliver a cast of characters, plot, and a crashing climax all in the span of two or three minutes. Take that, *Young and the Restless.*

X-TINCTION RATING: Still going strong. As long as country music lives, the story song will never die.

Strawberry Shortcake

THE dregs of a fruit smoothie left to curdle on your car's dashboard in July. Fruit preserves soaked in cheap perfume. A melted gel air freshener. That's probably not what the chemists at American Greetings had in mind, but that's kind of what Strawberry Shortcake dolls smelled like. There was a hint of something that suggested fruit, but it was quickly overwhelmed by that plasticky, chemically aroma.

But buying Strawberry Shortcake dolls for the scent was like buying Chanel No. 5 for the texture. The smelly little family appealed most to girls hanging on the cusp between Fisher-Price and Barbie. And the dolls' names were so sugary they made your teeth ache: Strawberry's buddies included Blueberry Muffin, Lemon Meringue, and baby Apple Dumplin'. Most everyone had a cutely named pet, too, including Custard the cat and Pupcake the dog. No one was named Multi-Grain Breadbunny.

So many questions surround the Strawberry Shortcake world. Why was a greeting-card company making dolls? (Answer: Cash. Strawberry Shortcake reportedly generated more than $1 billion in retail sales between 1980 and 1985.) Were you supposed to sniff them *while* playing with them? (Answer: It was impossible not to.) And if Strawberry Shortcake grew up and mated with boyfriend Huckleberry Pie, whose scent would the baby have? (Answer: Ugh.)

X-TINCTION RATING: Revised and revived.
REPLACED BY: After 1985, the dolls faded from the scene, but they've kept growing back, with new dolls, DVDs, websites, and even a 2006 big-screen release, *Strawberry Shortcake: The Sweet Dreams Movie*.

Stretch Armstrong

WITH his little wrestler's underpants and uncanny resemblance to Malibu Ken on 'roids, Stretch Armstrong was the centerpiece of Kenner's line of contortionist action figures that encouraged kids to pursue careers as either massage therapists or medieval torturers. Pulled to within an inch of his life or tied up in knots, the resilient Stretch always squiggled his way back to his original shape.

Stretch Armstrong's one weakness was anything sharper than a marshmallow. A single fingernail jab or poke with a pencil, and the muscular-yet-mushy man's latex skin would tear faster than a scab off a knee. Out poured a viscous goo—that's corn syrup to you and me—in a glacier-paced eruption of nontoxic sludge. More than one kid opened the lid of his toy box to find a surprisingly gaunt Stretch drowning in a slow-moving sea of his own innards. The wounds could be temporarily staunched with a Band-Aid, but most kids realized pretty quickly that a bleeding Stretch Armstrong was a delicious Stretch Armstrong. And if you claim to never have tasted Stretch's sweet, syrupy middle, then you, sir, are a liar.

X-TINCTION RATING: Revised and revived.

REPLACED BY: Post-Stretch, all sorts of elastic creatures slithered onto toy store shelves, from superheroes to octopi to Stretch X-Ray, a see-through alien. Kenner reintroduced Stretch Armstrong in the 1990s and added a new canine pal, the cleverly named Fetch Armstrong.

Sun-In

TODAY, some moms are willing to take even preteen girls to hair salons for highlights, but not in our day. Like Scarlett O'Hara pinching her cheeks to redden them because rouge was forbidden, teens who wanted to see if blondes really had more fun had to get creative. Lemon juice was the old standby, but a less sticky and time-consuming way to try to go blond was by using spray-on Sun-In.

And if a little was good, a lot was better. Girls marinated their locks in the stuff, then flopped onto a lawn chair and let the sun do its work. It was a very personal at-home science experiment, and it often failed miserably. The darker your hair was, the less effective the product. Orangey Sun-In streaks were as common as zits at some high schools, and the memory of its chemical smell lingers in the mind, and locker, of many a now-grown teenage girl.

X-TINCTION RATING: Still going strong.

FUN FACT: One of the product's slogans was "Sun-In and sunlight, and you'll be blonder tonight."

Sunshine

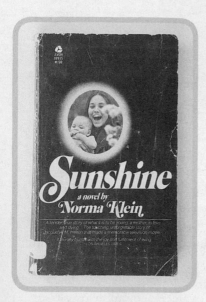

GIRLS of the 1970s and 1980s loved sad stories—just look to the popularity of *The Other Side of the Mountain* (skiing-caused paralysis) or *Ice Castles* (ice skating–induced blindness). But before those stories hit screens, there was the heartbreaking book *Sunshine*, about the short life of cancer-stricken teen mom Jacquelyn Helton (called Kate Hayden in the book). Author Norma Klein based her 1974 novel on tape-recorded diaries the real Helton kept as she struggled with the disease that started in her leg and took her life at age twenty.

It was *Love Story* with hippies instead of Harvardites, plus a motherless toddler. If your paperback wasn't tearstained by the part where the heroine says she can't learn to walk on one leg while her daughter is learning to walk on two, you clearly had a heart of stone.

Sunshine was later turned into an equally devastating TV movie and a short-lived series, which used "Sunshine on My Shoulders" as its haunting theme song. Today the book is hard to come by, and videotapes of the TV movie and series are impossible to find. But if you ever catch a woman bawling while the elevator Muzak plays a certain John Denver song, this may be the reason.

X-TINCTION RATING: Gone for good.

REPLACED BY: *Sunshine* is all but forgotten, but the tearjerker love story will never die. Just ask fans of *The Time Traveler's Wife*.

Super 8 Moviemaking

S WEET Spielberg, getting our hands on a Super 8 movie camera set our inner film geek free. What other artistic outlet let a kid build a dinosaur out of Play-Doh and animate it, frame by frame, so the little green guy lumbered herky-jerky across the floor? Suck on that, Crayola.

In our pre-VCR world, we could even film something off the TV and watch it any time we wanted! In theory, at least. Somewhere in a shoe box lies a reel of the opening credits of *Love Boat*, abandoned when we realized it wasn't worth the effort of setting up a projector and giant white screen just to watch thirty seconds of Gopher and Captain Stubing staring at the camera.

No iMovie, no YouTube. We sliced the film with a razor blade and painstakingly taped two pieces together, then repeated the process for every edit. We arranged showings of our masterpieces, cutting tickets out of construction paper and burning our fingers on the projector bulb. The movies may have been silent, but from the *flap flap flap* of the reel as it fluttered to a finish, to the *clap clap clap* of our parents as we proudly took our bows, it all still sounded like satisfaction to us.

X-TINCTION RATING: Gone for good.

REPLACED BY: Today, many kids have easy access to digital video cameras, but very few use them to stop-animate Play-Doh dinosaurs.

Super Friends

I T was as if DC Comics had been taken over by *Highlights* magazine. These were not the Superman, Batman, and Wonder Woman of your comic books; instead, dumbed down for younger audiences by Hanna-Barbera, they were superhero stories that John-Boy Walton might tell—violence-free and oh-so-wholesome.

Frustrations: Wonder Woman was clearly visible while flying in her invisible jet. Aquaman was completely helpless unless the current world-domination plot took place underwater. Batman and Robin had any tool at their disposal with the word "Bat" in front of it. When the series decided to diversify, it did so in a weirdly racist way—using Black Vulcan's very name to point out that he was black, something that was never done with, say, "White Aquaman."

Don't get us started on Marvin, Wendy, and Wonderdog, and their alien replacements Zan, Jayna, and that stupid monkey, Gleek. Annoying as they were, they did get kids running around the playground bumping fists and yelling "Wonder Twin Powers, activate!" Jayna's animal-transformation skill had potential, but she constantly used it to turn into lame things like woodpeckers. Zan's water-changing power was even stupider, especially when he insisted on turning into an ice trapeze or, worse, smiling water in a bucket. It's as if they chose their transformations via Mad Libs.

X-TINCTION RATING: Gone for good.

REPLACED BY: The superheroes retired to the comic pages where they belonged, and we can only hope the teen sidekicks were swiftly and mercilessly killed.

Sweet Valley High

JESSICA and Elizabeth Wakefield were the Goofus and Gallant of 1980s teen books. The average reader envied sassy cheerleading captain Jessica but was secretly more like Liz, the saintly school newspaper editor whose boyfriend, bland Todd Wilkins, was as dangerous as a saltine.

The books themselves were so ploddingly similar they all but demanded a drinking game. The twins' "silky blond hair and blue-green eyes" are mentioned? Drink! There's a reference to their "perfect size-six figures"? Drink! A reader has to go look up the word "lavaliere" because it's mentioned the twins wear matching ones? CHUG! (It's just a necklace, by the way. Not even made out of lava. Rip. Off.)

Liz and Jess were as likely to be kidnapped as attend class. Any new friends were the equivalent of red-shirted *Star Trek* ensigns,

introduced strictly to reveal a drug addiction, an eating disorder, or a secret psychosis before being washed away on a wave of Liz's moral righteousness. This awesomeness carried on for 150-plus books, including the *Sweet Valley Kids* and *Sweet Valley University* series. But sadly, we never got to see the inevitable *Sweet Valley Divorcées*, as a new generation dumped the twins for vampires and Harry Potter.

X-TINCTION RATING: Revised and revived.

REPLACED BY: The twins are suddenly popular again. A 2011 book, *Sweet Valley Confidential*, looks at Jess and Liz in their mid-twenties. And Oscar-winning screenwriter Diablo Cody, a longtime fan, is adapting the books into a movie.

FUN FACT: The twins' "perfect size-six" figures apparently weren't so perfect after all. When the books were reissued in 2008, the reference was changed to a size four.

Taco Bell BellBeefer

YES, the Mexican fast-food chain whose slogan later became "Think outside the bun" once thought inside the bun was a mighty fine place to be. We like to think the BellBeefer (originally named the Bell Burger, which was pretty Bell Boring) was invented one day when a frantic franchise ran out of taco shells. Really, it was just the contents of a regular beef taco—beef, sauce, onions, lettuce, and cheese—dumped onto a soft white hamburger bun, kinda like a Mexican sloppy Joe. But somehow the hot meat and fixings melted the wimpy bun into sheer junk-food perfection, the perfect cross-cultural marriage.

Kids from meat-and-potatoes homes who thought a tortilla was too daring, or those who really, really loved their school cafeteria chili burgers, weren't the only ones who ordered them. BellBeefers developed a cult following but, sadly, not enough of one to keep them around. However, the name lived on for years in certain circles, where it served as slang for either "vomit" or "fart," depending on your class of friend.

X-TINCTION RATING: Gone for good.
REPLACED BY: We've heard a rumor that some California Taco Bells still serve the BellBeefer. Will it ever return franchise-wide? Hey, the Enchirito made a comeback. Yo quiero keep dreaming.

Thriller

JUST try and keep still when the opening bars of Michael Jackson's "Billie Jean" or "Beat It" come on the radio. Wasn't possible in 1982, when *Thriller* first came out, and it's not any more realistic now. Even the klutziest kid on the block just had to crank up these tunes and move his feet like they were on fire.

Thriller was our *Sgt. Pepper*. Not owning a copy was like not owning lungs. Maybe you started with vinyl, then replaced it with a cassette for the boombox, then, after Jackson died in 2009, finally upgraded to CD. We knew every song, mouthed every lyric, merrily screeched right up into falsetto along with Michael. This was the soundtrack to proms, play rehearsals, basketball games, make-out sessions in Mom's old Bonneville. Untangling their notes from your memories would be like throwing away your yearbook.

Jackson was already famous, but *Thriller*'s release swept him up on a fame wave so massive that his sad end was all but foretold. But back on the *Thriller* album cover, he hadn't yet made that jump. Resting on one elbow, he looks young and nervous, like he's just asked for a date and is playing it cool while awaiting a response. What do you say, pretty young thing? Do you wanna be startin' somethin'?

X-TINCTION RATING: Still going strong.

FUN FACT: *Thriller* misheard lyrics are almost as awesome as the real words, and include "Billie Jean is not my brother," "No one's gonna save you from the bees about to bite," and "It's Phyllis Diller, Diller Night!"

Tickle Antiperspirant

IT'S not easy to differentiate one antiperspirant from another. They all smell vaguely floral, they all do pretty much the same thing. So Tickle burst out of the gate in the 1970s and went after its female audience with the coolest looking antiperspirant bottle ever seen. It featured a giant rollerball on a curvy pedestal base that was encased in a clear, polka-dotted sleeve. You could slip off the sleeve, and it was almost like you had a little pop-art sculpture right there on your bathroom counter.

The commercials were vaguely sexual, which was possibly unavoidable thanks to the shape of the bottle. It was apparently considered too personal to show a model actually putting on the product, kind of like how *The Brady Bunch* shot entire scenes in the bathroom without ever showing the toilet. So instead a model's carefully manicured finger was shown rolllllling over Tickle's enormous, um, ball. Kids couldn't help but copy the maneuver, which led to that finger inevitably finding its way into their mouths, which meant that most of Generation X probably ingested waaaay more Tickle than could possibly be healthy. At least we knew our tongues weren't going to break out in a sweat.

X-TINCTION RATING: Gone for good.
REPLACED BY: Tickle is gone, and our store shelves are the poorer for it. Sorry, Secret, you just aren't nearly as artistic to look at.
FUN FACT: A young Meg Ryan appears in one Tickle commercial, doing chin-ups and then dissolving into giggles.

Tiffany Taylor Doll

TWO, two, two dolls in one! In the 1970s, doll makers shook off the constraints of plain old Barbie and branched out into Wacky World. Blythe dolls changed their eye color! Crissy dolls changed their hair length! And along came Tiffany Taylor, who combined the two and let little girls change her hair color.

Now, girls had changed their dolls' hair color for years, but that process usually began with Magic Markers or Easter egg dye and ended with parental screaming fits and kids getting grounded. Tiffany made it acceptable. Her skull spun around to switch her hair from platinum blond to dark brunette, perfect for the kid who couldn't decide if Jill or Kelly was her favorite Charlie's Angel. (A black version of the doll offered black or coppery auburn hair.)

As cool as the two-tone hair sounded, Tiff had more issues than a *Seventeen* magazine subscription. Kids could intentionally spin her head just halfway and make her look as if she'd been horribly injured in an industrial mangler accident. Even when her hair was carefully swiveled to show the preferred shade, the other color was still obvious, making her look like a skunk, a punker, or the worst hair colorist on the planet. But kids didn't care because, hey, two dolls in one.

X-TINCTION RATING: Gone for good.

REPLACED BY: Tiffany was superseded by her little sister, Tuesday Taylor, who was just eleven inches tall to Tiffany's mega-giant nineteen inches.

Tim Conway/ Don Knotts Movies

QUICK—how many movies did Don Knotts and Tim Conway appear in together? Eighty? A hundred? Nope, just six. If it felt like the pair showed up in nearly every '70s-era kids' comedy, it was for good reason. Abbott and Costello and Laurel and Hardy were our parents' and grandparents' comedy teams; Knotts and Conway were all ours. We knew them well from TV, and somehow they became even more than the sum of their parts when they teamed up on the big screen. Conway was a dim-witted goof; Knotts barely contained his frustration at his buddy's shenanigans, letting it squeak out in double-takes, pursed lips, and dismissive sniffs. Together, comedy gold.

And what better way to while away an afternoon than watching those two knuckleheads engage in cinematic slapstick? After a pair of *Apple Dumpling Gangs* and a few lesser flicks, they hit their stride in *The Private Eyes*, the Sherlock Holmes spoof that set the pair loose in a spooky castle filled with hidden passages and opportunities to goof around. Just try not to pee yourself during the scene when Knotts fights back the barf while Conway lists off gross things like "warm milk with lard in it."

Our grandparents can keep their black-and-white memories of Hope and Crosby and Burns and Allen. We had Barney Fife and Dorf.

X-TINCTION RATING: Gone for good.
REPLACED BY: Sorry, Will Ferrell and John C. Reilly; we knew

Conway and Knotts, we loved Conway and Knotts, and you're no Conway and Knotts.

Time for Timer

TV was pretty lecturey in the 1970s and 1980s. Somewhere along the line, someone panicked that kids weren't eating proper snacks and decided the way to solve that was to offer nutritional advice from a yellow blob of fat with spindly legs and a ginormous hat. Thus, the birth of Timer, a disturbing but memorable PSA star whose segments were apparently dashed off by a bored but starving copywriter who had to make deadline before he could hit the drive-thru for a Big Mac.

Timer's most memorable video has him "hankering for a hunka cheese," but any kid who needed to be shown how to place cheese between two crackers was really too dumb to be allowed to watch TV. In another, Timer takes a tour of the stomach and then apparently just gives up, encouraging kids to eat random leftovers out of the fridge. "Sunshine on a Stick" oversells the result by half, as it's just orange juice frozen in ice-cube trays. Timer also shows up in a segment demonstrating toothbrushing, which is odd when you consider that his teeth are as yellow as the rest of him.

X-TINCTION RATING: Gone for good.
REPLACED BY: Nothing. Television networks have since decided that kids can eat random food out of the fridge without frightening cartoon guidance.

Time Life Books

OWBOYS, goblins, lost civilizations! Time Life Books read like encyclopedias with all the boring stuff cut out. Their extra-long TV commercials were mini-movies, letting us imagine joining the James Gang or plundering with the Vikings. We'd plead with our parents to call the 800 number and set the once-every-other-month delivery machine into motion. "Please, Mom? You get to examine it free for ten days!"

In one ad, Vincent Price pitched the *Enchanted World* series as books that "let you fly along with those unlucky spirits condemned to haunt the world of the living." Commercials for the *Old West* series told kids about gunslinger John Wesley Hardin, who was "so mean, he once shot a man just for snoring."

But what really set the books apart was less the content and more the elaborate bindings. The *Enchanted World* series was bound in fabric; the *Old West* version had "the look and feel of hand-tooled saddle leather." Our Scholastic Book Club paperbacks looked sad by comparison.

We wish the line had endured, just to see what Time Life would have tried next. Would a series on food have been bound in real cheese slices? But alas, the books eventually ended up in garage sales all over the country when people finally realized that they were indeed good-looking on the outside but less than useful in daily life. Apparently, you can't judge a book by its cover after all.

X-TINCTION RATING: Gone for good.
REPLACED BY: Time Life now focuses on CDs and DVDs. Infomercials have featured Kevin Cronin of REO Speedwagon hawking

a collection of power rock ballads and Billy Dee Williams pitching the music of Motown.

Toy Catalogs

FORGET cookies and caroling—one of the best parts of Christmas was snuggling up on the couch with a department-store catalog. You'd skip past the endless pages of boring clothes and home furnishings, narrowing right in on the toys. It was so much better than a trip to the mall—no hot coats and slushy boots, no crowds, no Dad dragging you off to look at snow tires instead of Snoopy Sno-Cone Machines.

And we never even saw half these catalog treasures in our local stores. Superman-themed Big Wheels? Sing Along with Shaun Cassidy record players? Toy kitchens that were bigger than Mom's, *Starsky and Hutch* walkie-talkies, a four-story *Star Wars* space station that rivaled Barbie's Dream House for luxury?

Some sections gave you a peek at your own imagined future, when Mom might actually splurge on a pinball machine or trust you to play with Creepy Crawler goop. And still other pages puzzled. Was there that much call for Donny and Marie marionettes, and who were the kids buying all these chemistry sets and microscopes?

Here's the thing about toy catalogs: They taught you about life. You knew you weren't going to get everything you wanted, but surely some of your dreams would come true. For the rest of it, sometimes just knowing it was out there was enough.

X-TINCTION RATING: Gone for good.

Transistor Radios

CALLIN' out around the world, we were ready for a brand-new beat. The portable, battery-powered marvels that were transistor radios allowed us to dance in the streets to our very own soundtracks. Finally, we could listen to Night Ranger wherever and whenever we damn well pleased—including, if we hid the tiny earpiece behind our feathered hairdos, in class.

The radio designs were pop-art pizzazz—there were giant dice, Coke bottles, Folger's cans, even ladybugs with dials for eyes. Kids dragged around the colorful ball-shaped Panapet by its chain, a futuristic dog that barked staticky Barry Manilow songs. The Toot-A-Loop was shaped like a pregnant bagel. Part high-tech party starter, part fashion accessory, it could be worn around the wrist or twisted into a mod "S" shape. Try doing that with a record player.

On clear nights, we thumbed the ribbed little dial and surfed the airwaves, tuning in broadcasts from exotic cities hundreds or even thousands of miles away. It was a window into another world—a snowed-in kid in St. Paul could drift to sleep listening to a Dallas DJ drawl on about how hot it was. We'd feel like high-tech eavesdroppers, listening to voices from towns we'd never been to talk about traffic on highways we'd never ever drive on. What's the frequency, Kenneth? Pure broadcasting bliss.

X-TINCTION RATING: Gone for good.
REPLACED BY: Remember your SAT analogies? Transistor radios are to today's MP3 players as typewriters are to laptops. What sounded so cool then seems unmanageably clunky now.

Trapper Keepers

THE world of school supplies was pretty stagnant until 1978, when Mead introduced the Trapper Keeper and really upped the coolness ante. The folders, or Trappers, came with wraparound flaps that held your papers in even if the class bully knocked them to the floor. And they were punched with three holes so that the Trappers could all hang out together in your Trapper Keeper, a binder with snappy sliding plastic rings and a rip-r-iffic Velcro closure. Even if all you were organizing were drawings of your dream bedroom, complete with secret passageway, escalator, and soft-serve ice-cream machine, you felt positively tycoonlike with your Trapper Keeper stuffed under your arm.

The first Trapper Keepers we remember were in simple solid colors—turquoise was a favorite—but soon the designs were flying fast and furious. A Saint Bernard carrying a bucket of flowers. A baby harp seal cuteing it up on an ice floe. Kittens. Swans. Hot sports cars. Paint splatters. Scenes that seemed to represent either a futuristic city or the inner workings of a pinball machine. Kids too old to wear their sentiments on a metal lunch box transferred them to the Trapper Keeper instead. It didn't mean your homework was any better, but it certainly was organized.

X-TINCTION RATING: Revised and revived.
REPLACED BY: Mead brought out a new version of the Trapper Keeper in 2007, replacing the Velcro with magnetic or snap closures.

TV Theme Songs

WONDERING how the seven SS *Minnow* passengers found their way to Gilligan's Island? Just sit right back and you'll hear a tale! Confused as to how Greg and Marcia were related? Here's the story . . . of a lovely lady!

Some theme songs required that you know a tiny bit about the plot, so you could figure out why Chico shouldn't get discouraged, or just how Wonder Woman got into her satin tights, fighting for our rights. Others were so subtle that they actually charted—*Kotter*'s bouncy "Welcome Back" could have been about any dreamer returning home, and *Greatest American Hero*'s peppy "Believe It or Not" resonated with anyone who couldn't believe their luck. ("It should've been somebody ellllllllllse!") And some shows appeared to have written a theme song, then said "Aw, to hell with it" and had an actor speak the words instead. ("Now they work for me. My name is Charlie.")

Good theme songs essentially served as catchy jingles promoting their shows—ads that viewers carried around in their heads. Ask any kid hopscotching to "Schlemiel! Schlimazel!" on the playground, or trying to decipher what Archie and Edith were singing around the piano. (It was "Gee our old LaSalle ran great.") Themes were the musical wrapping for a sitcom present—not really necessary but surprisingly missed once they started to disappear. They could take a nothing show and suddenly make it all seem worthwhile.

X-TINCTION RATING: Gone for good.
REPLACED BY: Sure, you'll still find an occasional explanatory TV theme, kind of. ("Lucky there's a Family Guy!") But the cooler trend is to pick a song that already exists and make the show own it—think Tony Soprano driving home to "Woke Up This Morning, Got Myself a Gun."

Typing Class

HIGH school in the '80s was dangerous. You could sand off your skin in shop class, burn your buns in home ec, and risk severe finger injury in typing. Computers were still a futuristic dream, and working with newfangled electric typewriters was like learning to fly the space shuttle.

You'd flip on the IBM Selectric or Smith-Corona, and it'd leap to life with a loud *ka-chink* and sustained hum. You'd press a key, and the typewriter would respond with a gunshotlike crack. Press too hard, and the "W" would WWWWWWWWWWWWWWWWWWW its way across the page before you even knew what was happening.

Accidentally rest your hand on the Return key, and the paper would shoot up like a bright white piece of toast.

No amount of repetitive exercise ("AAA space, SSS space, DDD space") was going to help us master this crazy piece of equipment. It was as if they'd set us in front of an industrial drill press and told us to build a car chassis. So we cautiously hunted and pecked as the teacher suspiciously cased the room, taking points off our score—or, worse, knocking our knuckles with a ruler—when she caught us looking at the keys.

Little did any of us know that all of those lessons would end up crumpled in the trash bin of history. Soon enough, thanks to Black-Berrys, we'd all be typing with our thumbs.

X-TINCTION RATING: Gone for good.
REPLACED BY: Schools today now offer "keyboardinq" classes. *Grade* schools, that is.
FUN FACT: In a 1976 episode of *Columbo*, the rumpled detective catches a murderer after discovering his motive imprinted on a used electric-typewriter ribbon.

Underoos

THE slogan said it all: "It's underwear that's fun to wear!" True, but what the Fruit of the Loom marketing department didn't mention was that Underoos were also underwear that could get you a severe beat-down if locker-room bullies caught a glimpse as you were changing for gym class.

Safely hidden under clothing, though? Underrific. Before you tore off the Christmas wrapping paper, they felt like a package of cotton disappointment (aka tighty-whities). But once you realized that they were the real deal—a colorful top emblazoned with a bat symbol or "S" insignia, and briefs, often with the waistband made to look like a belt—no amount of parental pleading could stop you from donning them right there in the living room. These super skivvies made kids feel exactly like comic-book heroes Superman, Batman, Wonder Woman, the Hulk, and Spider-Man. Except, of course, for the fact that Spidey's costume didn't have a wiener hole.

No matter what your mom made you wear on the outside, with Underoos on underneath, you knew you were always ready to rip off your Garanimals and fight crime at a moment's notice—like a third-grade Clark Kent. Underwear has never been so super.

X-TINCTION RATING: Still going strong.

FUN FACT: Fruit of the Loom still makes them, and now kids get their choice of boxers or briefs. Sadly, no more Princess Leia and Pac-Man, but SpongeBob and Dora the Explorer are popular options.

Unsafe Playground Equipment

ANY kid who played on a 1970s playground should kiss the feet of whoever invented the tetanus shot. Before child-safe equipment became the norm, metal, sharp, and dangerous were the order of the day. Pinched fingers, skinned knees, broken bones, amputations. Hundreds of kids laid out like the Civil War triage scene from *Gone with the Wind*. Injury was simply the price you paid for having fun.

Who didn't get their fingers trapped between metal links in the chain holding the swing? Blood blisters for everybody! Rickety ladders and seesaws with weather-beaten wood were giant slivers waiting to happen. Metal slides were surface-of-the-sun broiling; if you stopped halfway down, you'd have griddle marks on your butt. Slides were also prone to rusting away, and if you made the mistake of running your fingers along the jagged, brown sides, you'd end up with a handful of pain. Old-school merry-go-rounds could whip around in such a frenzy, kids would fly off and hit the side of the school. Or at the very least, their blood and internal organs would be relocated to one side of their body for the rest of recess.

X-TINCTION RATING: Revised and revived.

REPLACED BY: Although you can still find an occasional death trap of fun in a crummy park near you, the dangerous equipment has mostly been replaced by far safer alternatives, giving emergency room doctors a little more time off.

Variety Shows

SEVENTIES kids were too young to meet the Beatles on *Ed Sullivan*, but that doesn't mean we weren't inundated with TV variety shows. It was a familiar genre to any kid who'd ever attended a school talent show—people you knew put on gaudy costumes and sang, danced, and cracked jokes. And just as in a school talent show, some stars were naturals at it, while others made you wish you were Jamie Farr wielding a giant mallet on *The Gong Show*.

On any school playground, you could find kids trying to imitate Carol Burnett's awesome Tarzan yell. If Burnett was the cool mom of the genre, Sonny & Cher were the slightly frightening parents of your best friend. Sure, they were nice enough to you, but their digs at each other seemed devised to really draw blood.

Variety shows came and went so frequently it was really tough to keep up. Was it *The Brady Bunch Hour* or *Donny & Marie* that opened with ice skating, and which one had synchronized swimming? Was it the Carpenters or Captain and Tennille who ran their segments in alphabetical order? Even the Starland Vocal Band had a variety show. But the weirdest variety show to date, *Pink Lady and Jeff*, lasted all of four weeks, which seems kind of long considering two of its three stars barely spoke English.

X-TINCTION RATING: Gone for good.

REPLACED BY: The variety genre is a tough one to resurrect, but that doesn't stop people from occasionally trying. Rosie O'Donnell's *Rosie Live* was canceled after one 2008 episode. Maybe she should have added synchronized swimmers.

V. C. Andrews Books

I F Mom thought Judy Blume was bad, hoo boy, it's a good thing she didn't know about V. C. Andrews. Sure, Blume's *Forever* talked about sex, but Andrews's *Flowers in the Attic* talked about sex WITH YOUR BROTHER.

Yeah. Um. Gross. But thankfully, Andrews's characters were so rip-roaringly over the top that it was impossible to take them seriously. They had names like Heaven Leigh, Rain, and Ice, and were as breathtakingly beautiful as they were indistinguishable. Andrews (and her prolific ghostwriter) thought up exquisite tortures for them, the kind of thing that made us shudder but never stop reading. Eating rats! Drinking blood! Whippings! And we devoured the stories as if they were the arsenic-powdered donuts served up by Cathy and Chris's unbelievably evil grandmother.

The covers were shiny, dark, and menacing, with an actual hole cut into each one so that our heroine's angelic face could peer out, begging us to read her story and save her from a life of starvation and hot tar poured in her hair.

Why did we seek out such horrific tales? Most of us lived pretty standard suburban lives, where the biggest trauma was a pimple or a flunked test. We might have hated our parents for grounding us, but hey, at least we weren't starving to death in an attic. No matter how bad we thought we had it, Andrews's heroines always one-upped us.

X-TINCTION RATING: Still going strong, thanks to a ghostwriter who picked up after Andrews died in 1986.
FUN FACT: V. C. Andrews was really C. V. Andrews—her name was Cleo Virginia.

Videos on MTV

ONCE upon a time, the "M" in MTV stood for "music." Now we're pretty sure it stands for "mediocre reality-show stars." Once Puck from *The Real World* and Johnny Knoxville from *Jackass* moved in, the cable channel apparently went deaf to its once-edgy and proud history.

MTV launched way back in 1981, and those of us who didn't have cable had to settle instead for NBC's once-a-week impersonator, *Friday Night Videos*. But eventually we all got our MTV, reveling in the thrill of seeing our favorite pop songs performed live, acted out in little playlets, or turned into wacky cartoons.

Just try to think of Michael Jackson's "Thriller" without picturing his zombie pals, "Take on Me" without A-ha's pencil-sketched lovers, or Robert Palmer's "Addicted to Love" without his sullen lady friends. Sure, some of the early videos seemed as though they were shot in an hour over lunch, but they laid the groundwork for a revolution in short-form storytelling and had a phenomenal impact on pop culture.

Back then, we weren't lying when we repeated MTV's simple but truthful tagline, "I want my MTV." Although now that the network has thrust *Jersey Shore* upon the world, we're honestly not so sure.

X-TINCTION RATING: Gone for good.
REPLACED BY: MTV does still play a few videos, but in 2010 it officially dropped "Music Television" from its name and logo. Now the web is the most music video–friendly frontier.
FUN FACT: Yes, everyone knows that the Buggles's "Video Killed the Radio Star" was MTV's first video. Not as many remember the second, however—it was Pat Benatar's "You Better Run."

View-Master

IN the 1978 Ward's Christmas catalog, View-Master took up two entire pages. That's twice as much space as a little phenomenon called *Star Wars*. You could buy the standard red plastic View-Master, but why would you? Other options included the theater-in-the-round View-Master, the rear-screen-projector View-Master, and the blue View-Master with its own light. And that just covered the viewers. Reels included generic science-class specials on such topics as sharks and prehistoric animals, classics like *Charlotte's Web*, travelogues from Disneyland to Detroit, and such TV faves as *CHiPs* and *Dark Shadows*.

Based on nineteenth-century stereograms, View-Masters first came out in the 1930s. Forty years later, everyone had one buried in a toy chest. In those days before you could watch the Apollo

moon landing footage over and over again on a computer, seeing it in View-Master's weirdly appealing 3-D, summarized into three snappy reels of seven images each, was just a little bit cool. Face it—you were always kind of sad when you clicked back around to the first picture.

Despite innovations like the talking version (for illiterate kids?) and the red, white, and blue bicentennial edition, these were never hip toys. Yet flipping through someone else's collection of reels was like nosing through their family photos combined with a quaint, outdated encyclopedia. Hey, they went to Cypress Gardens, too!

X-TINCTION RATING: Still going strong.
FUN FACT: DreamWorks is reportedly working on a View-Master big-screen movie.

Wacky Packages

WACKY Packages combined three of kids' favorite things: goofy commercial mascots, paint-peeling stickers, and really, really lame jokes.

Wacky creators never went for the subtle. Silly Putty became Killy Putty! Peter Pan peanut butter? Peter Pain! Spam? Cram! It's like the *Simpsons* episode where Marge suggests a pile of names for about-to-be-born Bart and Homer is ready with a stupid taunt for each. ("Marcus? They'll call him Mucus!")

But kids were not exactly looking for Thomas Pynchon. Obvious ruled in Wackyland, and Gross shared the throne. Who could resist a bucket of the Colonel's finest when it was renamed Kentucky Fried Fingers? Crest toothpaste became garlic-flavored Crust. A horrified housewife shrieked as she cooked up a batch of Minute Lice.

Let that nice girl next door gussy up her notebook with Snoopy and scratch 'n' sniff strawberries; you were rebelling against the advertising establishment, even if you weren't quite sure what it was. Pass the Frosted Snakes.

X-TINCTION RATING: Revived and revised.

REPLACED BY: Wacky Packs are back, Jack! Topps is once again cranking out new parodies ("Dead Bull no-energy drink") while also paying homage to their retro legacy. Wacky Packs Old School features new stickers parodying old 1970s products, while Wacky Pack Flashbacks reprint actual 1970s Wackys.

The Watcher in the Woods

I F you're inexplicably freaked out by mirrors, blindfolds, eclipses, and backwards writing on foggy windows, perhaps it's because you once saw Disney's most disturbing kid movie ever, 1980's *Watcher in the Woods*. It starred the girl from *Ice Castles* (Lynn-Holly Johnson) and a completely desiccated Bette Davis. In a fabulous movie coincidence, *Ice Castles* girl just happened to look like Davis's character's daughter, Karen, who'd mysteriously disappeared thirty years ago.

In one of the film's most-remembered creep-out scenes, *Ice Castles* girl's little sister gets all possessed and writes "NERAK"—"Karen" backwards—on a window. Her perfect backwards handwriting was so impressive that plenty of young viewers were inspired to attempt to do the same for weeks afterward on foggy school bus windows.

Many parents, lulled into security by Disney's blander live-action fare, foolishly let their kids see *Watcher* without realizing that nightmares would ensue. Forget mirrors and blindfolds, just staring at Bette Davis's sunken-in cheeks for an hour or so was pretty horrifying. Critics snorted that the movie never delivered, but (spoiler!)

Karen comes back safe in the end, which is more than *The X-Files* can say for Mulder's sister.

X-TINCTION RATING: Gone for good.
REPLACED BY: Sorry, Freddy and Jason, your murders are gruesome, but none of your films give us goose bumps the same way that *Watcher* did.
FUN FACT: The DVD features two alternate endings.

Waterbeds

THEY were slooshy, splorfy, and, for some reason, a vehicle for showcasing wildlife art. Waterbeds in the '70s and '80s were often capped by headboards with majestic elk etched into the mirrors, ornate dark-stained finials, and frosted-glass cupboard doors. Convenient cubbies allowed hipsters to show off their eight-track tape players, lava lamps, and giant ashtrays. Classy.

Waterbeds were mini *Poseidon Adventures* waiting to happen: When the inevitable leak came—and it always did—the stream would shoot high into the air, like a shopping-mall fountain, until you could get it patched. But it was the adults' job to fix the problem. Kids just loved the beds for their resemblance to a water park ride; we could hop on and surf, or pretend we commanded the SS *Serta*. It was the equivalent to having your very own blow-up bouncy house. Or, when it leaked, a Slip 'N Slide.

Adults seemed to enjoy them for, um, other reasons. We weren't exactly sure what was going on, but the sound of sloshing coming from the parents' bedroom when we slept overnight at a friend's house always made us seasick.

X-TINCTION RATING: Still going strong. OK, maybe not strong, but you can still get one if you look pretty hard.

FUN FACT: In a classic Snoopy strip, the hapless beagle can't get off a sloshing waterbed in time to catch the burglars robbing Peppermint Patty's house.

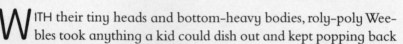

Weebles

WITH their tiny heads and bottom-heavy bodies, roly-poly Weebles took anything a kid could dish out and kept popping back up for more, like a punching bag with a weighted butt. As you may have gleaned from the annoying but unforgettable jingle, they wobbled but they didn't fall down.

They were Indians and pirates, ghosts and ringmasters, doggies and pigs. Even though their arms were stuck inside their eggy shell—and they didn't have any legs—Weebles certainly had fulfilling leisure lives, with accessories ranging from campers and haunted houses to circuses and submarines.

The skin on the earliest models tended to peel off, so Weeble manufacturer Playskool encased later versions in clear plastic shells. Although the plastic looked protective, kids quickly found that heat, water, and dirt could still get inside. If you dropped a Weeble in the sink to see if it could swim, or sent it on a trip through the dishwasher, the outside would stay intact but the inside . . . eew. There's something unsettling about a little cowboy slowly shriveling away, as if it had toy leprosy.

X-TINCTION RATING: Still going strong.

FUN FACT: For a while there, Playskool cranked out Weebles that were only vaguely egg-shaped, with—disturbingly—fully formed upper bodies, including arms. But in 2010, the original little oval guys returned.

William Zabka

THERE were plenty of pretty-boy bullies in '80s movies, but all of their blond hairdos, snarky smirks, and dripping sarcasm combined didn't add up to one William Zabka.

There was nobody better at capturing seething entitlement and impatience with nerds than Zabka, who stalked the screen awash in testosterone and, probably, Brut aftershave. The second he stepped into frame, audiences knew that Zabka would be the one to root against, and nowhere was that more apparent than when he played Cobra Kai Johnny Lawrence in *The Karate Kid*. Whether he was chasing Ralph Macchio while dressed as a skeleton, or sweeping Daniel-san's injured leg during the climactic competition, Zabka nailed the jock-with-a-chip-on-his-shoulder role, while subtly infusing him with a bit of humanity. Which made him even scarier.

Zabka could have hung it up after *Karate Kid*, content in the fact that he'd aced a spot in the Movie Villain Hall of Fame. But he continued to ride his wave of evil through the '80s, menacing Rodney Dangerfield's son (and wearing a red Speedo and caveman costume) in *Back to School* and terrorizing ninety-eight-pound weaklings in the cafeteria in *Just One of the Guys*.

Even we nerds had to admire his tenacity. All hail William Zabka, King of the Jerks.

X-TINCTION RATING: Still going strong.

FUN FACT: He's still acting. And believe it or not, moviedom's biggest bully was nominated for an Oscar in 2004 for *Most*, a film he produced and cowrote.

Willy Wonka & the Chocolate Factory

WAS 1971's *Willy Wonka & the Chocolate Factory* the weirdest kid movie of all time? Your Honor, the evidence:

Charlie Bucket's four decrepit grandparents share a bed while waiting for death. The acid trip of a boat ride where Wonka completely loses it. Violet Beauregard turns into a giant blueberry. And the smoking gun? The orange-faced, musically moralizing Oompa-Loompas. The prosecution rests.

Despite this sea of weirdness, and really, because of it, *Wonka* stuck with us all these years, like a watermelon Jolly Rancher on a molar. It's a scrumdiddlyumptious, imaginative ride through crazy-town. Gene Wilder's performance as candymaster Willy Wonka was a sweet little nugget of nougat covered in bitter—and demented—chocolate.

"You lose!" Wonka curtly lied to Charlie, just before he handed over the keys to the candy factory. But any kid who watched the thing won pretty big. Any kid but Violet, Veruca, Mike, and Augustus, that is. Wonka promised Charlie that the other children would be restored to their "normal, terrible old selves." We always suspected Wonka lied about that, too.

X-TINCTION RATING: Revised and revived.
REPLACED BY: Johnny Depp starred in *Charlie and the Chocolate Factory*, the 2005 version of the 1964 Roald Dahl book.
FUN FACT: IMDb.com reports that Jean Stapleton was the first choice to play Mike TeeVee's mom, but she chose to do the *All in the Family* pilot instead.

Wonka Oompas

P UT your prejudices about the scary orange-faced little guys aside. For one tasty part of the 1970s, Oompas was the name of a candy, and they were as magical as Everlasting Gobstoppers. Shaped a little like M&M's that had eaten too many M&M's, the candies somehow balanced two fillings, with peanut butter cream on top and chocolate on the bottom. Or vice versa, if you flipped your Oompa over.

Many an Oompa-loving kid felt cheated when Reese's Pieces came out in 1978. They looked like Oompas, and the word "Reese's" hinted at a PB and chocolate marriage, but one bite proved that wrong. The filling was all peanut butter, with the only chocolate found in the candy shell. Oompa, loompa, doompa-di-disappointing.

X-TINCTION RATING: Gone for good.

REPLACED BY: Wonka killed off Oompas, but resurrected the name for a fruity candy that resembled gumball-sized Skittles. Still pining for the original? Peanut butter M&M's come close, especially their Easter-only Speck-tacular Eggs, which wrap chocolate around a center of peanut butter. But true Oompas fans claim the texture of the peanut butter cream has never been replicated.

ZOOM

FORGET Pig Latin. The cool kid's language of the 1970s was Ubbi Dubbi ("Hub-i, Fr-ubiends!"), and if you could speak it, you felt like a genius and sounded like a dork. Most of us just faked it. But it was still one of the best parts of the kids' show *ZOOM*, which ran on PBS from 1972 to 1978.

ZOOM had a DIY feel long before we knew what DIY meant. The games Zoomers played had been sent in by real kids, so they felt random but real. No network legal department today would ever approve CrackerWhistle, where you and a friend stuff wads of saltines into your mouths and try to be the first to choke enough down so that you can whistle.

Some of *ZOOM*'s trademarks survived well after the show was canceled. What kid didn't try to copy the weird fluttery hand movements made by early Zoomer Bernadette? Or puzzle over the language game called Fannee Doolee? And forget 90210, the ZIP code kids knew best in the 1970s was "BOS-Ton Mass, OH-two-ONE-three-FOUR!"

It's a true American mystery that kids at recess in, say, Maine, often sing the same jump-rope rhymes or play the same clapping games as kids in Southern California or Seattle or Miami. Kid knowledge seems to spread through osmosis, but we'd bet a lot of it originated with an ever-changing cast in striped rugby shirts. Come on and Zoom Zoom Zoom-a Zoom . . .

X-TINCTION RATING: Gone for good.

REPLACED BY: A new version of *ZOOM* aired from 1999 to 2005.

FUN FACT: Bernadette's wacky arm motion is based on a sword dance her father learned in China. So many viewers wrote in asking about it that *ZOOM* had her teach it on the show.

ACKNOWLEDGMENTS

To properly acknowledge everyone who in some way contributed to this book, we'd have to go back in time and thank everyone who joined in our childhood pop-culture fun, whether they played the Dark Shadows board game with us or helped us stab Stretch Armstrong till we found out what was inside (Answer: Goo!). If you are one of those people, please consider yourself thanked.

Gael Fashingbauer Cooper would also like to thank Rob and Kelly Cooper; Ann, Ed, E.H., Claudia, Drew, and Dave Fashingbauer; Anne, Tom, Josh, and Sam Howard; Annie-marie and Mark Miller; April, Heidi, and Christian Fashingbauer; Clio, Carl, Maggie, Molly, and Erin McLagan; Grace and Paul Peters; Pete Cooper and Linda Richardson; Alison Cooper Valenziano; Todd Mannis; Lisa Olchefske Gilbert; Suzanne Dillon; Ann Simerson Williams; Bob Seabold and Bobbe Norenberg; Scott and Stacy Pampuch; Scott Feraro; Matt Gillen; Dan Dosen; Jeannine Walden Roberts; her Fashingbauer and Votel cousins; her Seattle book club posse; the Lenora Mattingly Weber list; Francine Ruley for loaning out some of her pop-culture collection; the entire Derham Hall High School class of 1985; and everyone who's ever read *Pop Culture Junk Mail* and *Gen X-tinct*.

Brian Bellmont would like to thank Jen, Rory, and Maddy

Bellmont; brothers Mike, Kevin, and especially Dave, for the generous use of his collection of nerd things; Mom and Dad; his grandparents, Bob and Jeanette Welle; Ryan Bisson; Molly Bellmont; Allison, Kelsey, Eric, and Al Guggisberg; Sue and Darwin Buerkle; Phyllis Iverson; childhood, high school, and college pop-culture partners-in-crime Andrew Leahy, Kevin Kasparek, and Chris Moore; Dave Nimmer, Dave Aeikens, Kathleen Hennessy, and Mike Zipko; kajillions of cousins, nieces, nephews, aunts, and uncles, especially Liz Hoch and Pete Welle; Aquinites, WEAUers, and Shandwickians; and classmates and teachers from Sts. Peter and Paul and Cathedral.

We would also like to thank our agent, Uwe Stender, and our more-awesome-than-Choco-Diles editor, Meg Leder.

PHOTO CREDITS

PHOTOGRAPHED items are from the authors' personal collections unless otherwise noted.

Atari: Clio McLagan
Barrel of Monkeys: Ensemble Creative & Marketing
Benji: Mulberry Square Productions Inc.
Big Wheel: Clio McLagan
Candy cigarettes: Ensemble Creative & Marketing
Charlie's Angels cards: Red Box Pictures
Choose Your Own Adventure cover: Chooseco LLC; *Space and Beyond*: Chooseco LLC.
Crissy: Beth Colvin, CrissyandBeth.com
Dapper Dan: Ensemble Creative & Marketing
Dynamite: Red Box Pictures
Fisher-Price Little People: Red Box Pictures
Free to Be . . . You and Me: Red Box Pictures
Funny Face: Red Box Pictures
Gee, Your Hair Smells Terrific: Red Box Pictures
G.I. Joe: Ensemble Creative & Marketing
Halloween masks: Clio McLagan
Hal Needham Stunt Set: Ensemble Creative & Marketing
Hugo: Ensemble Creative & Marketing
Love's Baby Soft: Red Box Pictures
Malibu Barbie: Red Box Pictures

Metal lunch box: Ensemble Creative & Marketing
Mr. Yuk: Pittsburgh Poison Center at the University of Pittsburgh Medical Center
Mystery Date: Red Box Pictures
A Nightmare on Elm Street (Freddy Krueger doll): Ensemble Creative & Marketing
O'Boisies: Red Box Pictures
The Osmonds cartoon show: Rankin/Bass Productions / Rick Goldschmidt Archives
Pepsi Light: Red Box Pictures
Pop Rocks: Red Box Pictures
Pop Shoppe: The Pop Shoppe
Pudding Pops: Ensemble Creative & Marketing
Quisp: Red Box Pictures
Rankin/Bass (Rudolph): Rankin/Bass Productions / Rick Goldschmidt Archives
Sassy: Red Box Pictures
Saturday Night Fever clothes: Bob and Karen Bellmont
Scratch 'n' sniff stickers: Red Box Pictures
Shrinky Dinks: K&B Innovations Inc. (USA)
Six Million Dollar Man: Ensemble Creative & Marketing
Sunshine: Red Box Pictures
Super 8 movies: Ensemble Creative & Marketing
Sweet Valley High: Red Box Pictures
Tiffany Taylor: Red Box Pictures
Transistor radio (Panapet): Ensemble Creative & Marketing
Underoos: Bob and Karen Bellmont
View-Master: Red Box Pictures
Wacky Packages: Red Box Pictures
Weebles: Ensemble Creative & Marketing

INDEX

★ 223

ABOUT THE AUTHORS

Gael Fashingbauer Cooper is a Twin Cities born-and-raised journalist who now lives in Seattle with her husband, Rob, and daughter, Kelly. USAToday.com named her one of the Top Pop Culture People of 2002. Her personal blog, *Pop Culture Junk Mail* (popculturejunkmail.com), dates to 1999. *Entertainment Weekly* named the site one of "100 Websites You Must Know Now," and the *New York Times* called it "one of the best places to explore pop culture online." She didn't exactly name her daughter after Kelly Garrett on *Charlie's Angels* or Kelly Leak from *The Bad News Bears*, but there may have been some influence.

Former TV news reporter and producer **Brian Bellmont** is a public relations consultant in the Twin Cities, where he lives with his wife, Jen, and daughters, Rory and Maddy. He's an award-winning food writer and aspiring novelist, and is a fan of all things pop culture, from horror flicks to comic books, Broadway musicals to beach reads, terrible sitcoms to *The Backyardigans*. Over the years, he's interviewed pop-culture staples like Adam West, Barry Williams, Loni Anderson, and Davy Jones; contributed to MSNBC.com and dozens of other media outlets; and written the copy on the back of a bag of yogurt-covered raisins.